Cities in Crisis:
The Urban Challenge in the Americas

Edited by
Matthew Edel
and
Ronald G. Hellman

*BILDNER
CENTER
FOR
WESTERN
HEMISPHERE
STUDIES*

The Graduate School and University Center of
The City University of New York

Library of Congress Cataloging-in-Publication Data

Cities in Crisis.

   Bibliography: p.
   1. Cities and towns—Latin America.   2. Latin American—
Social conditions—1945-   . I. Edel, Matthew. II. Hellman, Ronald G.
HT127.5.C577 1989   307.7'6'098   88-7475

ISBN 0-929972-03-1
ISBN 0-929972-04-X (paperback)

Cover, book design and layout by André Boucher
Manufactured in the United States of America
First Edition

CONTENTS

PREFACE

Cities in Crisis: The Urban Challenge in the Americas is the product of a Bildner Center research and colloquia series on the Urban Challenge in the Western Hemisphere. This project brings together leading urban scholars and policymakers from the United States, Latin America and the Caribbean to examine the problems of their cities, to share experience and to propose solutions. Many urban problems in the hemisphere are interdependent or suffered in common; this project has aimed at developing a hemispheric perspective and at enhancing international, inter-city cooperation. The essays in this volume were presented by their authors at colloquia sessions.

The Charles H. Revson Foundation funded the colloquia series in 1984-1985. The views expressed, however, are solely the responsibility of the authors. The Revson Foundation, which was established by the founder of Revlon, Inc. before his death in 1975, gives grants in the areas of urban affairs and public policy, with special emphasis on New York City; education; biomedical research policy; and Jewish education.

The Bildner Center for Western Hemisphere Studies sponsors research, forums, seminars and publications that address the practical resolution of public policy problems facing the nations of the hemisphere. It is part of The Graduate School and University Center of The City University of New York (CUNY). The Center serves as a link between CUNY's intellectual community and other experts and policymakers working on contemporary issues in Latin America, North America and the Caribbean, and provides a window on New York for scholars and public officials throughout the Americas. The Center was established in 1982 by the President of CUNY's Graduate School and University Center, the university's Board of Trustees, and Albert Bildner, a philanthropist with extensive experience in hemispheric affairs.

Urban Challenge in the Western Hemisphere

Chairman, International Advisory Panel	Ronald G. Hellman
Project Director	Matthew Edel
Project Coordinator	Felinda Mottino

Bildner Center Publications

General Editor	Ronald G. Hellman
Managing Editor	Sheila Klee
Editorial Researchers	Julio Chan-Sánchez
	David Sehr

CONTRIBUTORS

Matthew Edel — Urban Studies, Queens College;
Ph. D. Program in Economics,
Graduate School of CUNY

Ronald G. Hellman — Bildner Center
for Western Hemisphere Studies;
Ph. D. Program in Sociology,
Graduate School of CUNY

Vilmar Evangelista Faría — Department of Social Sciences,
Universidade Estadual de Campinas,
São Paulo

Orlandina de Oliveira — El Colegio de México
Mexico City

Humberto Muñoz García — Instituto de Investigaciones Sociales,
Universidad Nacional Autónoma de México
Mexico City

José Francisco Peña Gómez — Mayor, Santo Domingo, Dominican Republic
(1982-1986)

Elizabeth Jelin — Centro de Estudios de Estado y Sociedad
Buenos Aires

*Héctor Abad Gómez — Chairman of the Department of Preventive
Medicine and Public Health at the School of
Medicine, University of Antioquia
Medellín

Kathryn Stephens-Rioja — City and Regional Planning Department,
University of California, Berkeley

George Priestley — Political Science,
Queens College, CUNY

*Dr. Abad Gómez was assassinated in August, 1987, while he was President of
the Human Rights Committee and mayoral candidate in Medellín.

INTRODUCTION

Cities in Crisis: The Urban Challenge in The Americas

by
Matthew Edel and
Ronald G. Hellman

I
The Urban Challenge Series

The Bildner Center for Western Hemisphere Studies, at The Graduate School and University Center of The City University of New York (CUNY), was founded in 1982 to address common problems of North and South America, and to help the United States and Latin America learn from each other. As part of an urban university, it was inevitable that we would soon turn to urban concerns. Beginning in 1984, a series of colloquia on the urban challenge was funded by the Charles H. Revson Foundation, which has a history of supporting projects on New York City's problems. They accepted the Bildner Center's view that an exchange of ideas about common problems would be beneficial to cities in both the U.S. and in Latin America. The papers presented here were developed or presented in these colloquia. A core group including both New York-oriented urbanists and Latin Americanists, from CUNY and other New York institutions, took part in the colloquia. Other participants, including the authors of several of the papers, were invited to attend from Latin America. We extend special appreciation to Felinda Mottino for her important role in both the conceptual development of the project and in organizing the colloquia series.

The colloquia were designed to initiate a process of mutual learning. New York and its City University have developed a strong corps of urbanists, but many of these have limited their work to the United States, or to the developed Western-bloc nations. On the other hand, with a few exceptions, Latin Americanists have tended to specialize in national-level analyses of economic development and international relations, or in the study of agrarian problems. We felt that by having U.S.-centered urbanists and Latin American generalists meet and interact, we could stimulate more interest in Latin American cities.

Furthermore, most urban studies which had been done in Latin America in the 1970s had come to focus on two topics, either the overall distribution of population and the incentive to migrate, or the political organization of squatter housing settlements and other informal sector activities. Without diminishing the importance of these two topics, we wanted to examine issues which might affect cities in both of the Americas. What might seem to be traditional urban problems for the North American urbanist had been little-studied in Latin America. Thus we sought to focus on the formal political system and the position of the mayor; on the economic development and possible deindustrialization of urban regions; on suburban sprawl and metropolitan government; and on problems such as housing, public health, violence and environmental quality.

The original design for the seminars involved a choice of several of these "critical issues" areas and of several cities. The initial issues were to be economy, physical infrastructure, civic participation, housing, health and human resources, environment, city finance and planning and the quality of life. Each issue was to be looked at primarily through the experience of a different city.

In practice, however, issues proved difficult to keep separate. A session on civic participation also required attention to the economy; one on physical infrastructure turned out to focus on issues of civic participation and so on. Problems raised in one or another context came to repeat themselves. A discussion of governance in Santo Domingo and one on health in Medellín both raised issues of violence; sessions on the economy of São Paulo and on the quality of life in Buenos Aires both led to discussions of city and suburban jurisdiction over public services. This interconnectedness of problems did not really surprise us: as social scientists we are aware of the need for a holistic view. Nonetheless, reaching these common issues through discussions of different social or policy problems led to more concrete discussions than would papers attempting to cover all of the urban problems of one or more cities.

II
The Papers

In this volume, we present essays that deal with urban issues at two levels. The first is the economic or political overview. The chapters on São Paulo, by Vilmar Faría, and on Mexico City, by Orlandina de Oliveira and Humberto Muñoz, are overviews of the demographic and economic situations of those cities, but are informed by the authors' concerns for planning and political issues. Similarly, the talk on the problems of governing Santo Domingo, given by Mayor José Francisco Peña Gómez, and the essay on the New York fiscal crisis, by Matthew Edel, are focused on the government role, but also take an overview stance.

The other set of essays initially seems to focus on more detailed topics. Elizabeth Jelin reports how families in Buenos Aires survived economic and political crises. Hector Abad Gómez discusses public health in Medellín. Kathryn Stephens-Rioja focuses on housing in Mexico City. George Priestley analyzes popular mobilization and government in one municipality of the Panama City metropolis. But these essays lead the reader back to broader issues of how specific problems fit into the broader crisis.

Other discussions in the colloquium series, not presented here, included treatments of neighborhood renewal and public space in Havana; public service finance in Argentina; and ideologies of regionalism in Peru. A session on whether New York was becoming "more like" Third World cities is reported in Edel's paper. Our tentative conclusions, imparted here, are based both on the papers and on more general discussions within the group. These conclusions, overall, reinforce our initial impression that the cities of the "developed" North American "center" and those of the "less developed" Latin American "periphery" do have many common problems, despite crucial differences, and do have much to learn from each other. This mutual learning is particularly important because, despite excellent research and analysis of some aspects of the urban challenge, other aspects remain insufficiently studied.

III
The State of Western Hemisphere Research

Rapid and large-scale urban growth has become a universal phenomenon in the twentieth century. In 1900 only one country, Great Britain, could be regarded as principally urban. Today all industrial societies are highly urbanized, and less developed countries also have rapidly growing urban populations. This has resulted in some important changes throughout the Western Hemisphere. Currently a majority of the population in both the United States and Latin America live in urban centers of more than 20,000 inhabitants. In Latin America the urban population grew from less than 50% in 1960 to 64.1% in 1979, with an overall growth rate of 4.2% for the 1960 to 1979 period. (Wilkie and Haber, 1981)

Projections of future urban population growth in the United States suggest that by the year 2000 approximately 90% of the people will be living within existing metropolitan regions (Butler, 1977). Even more dramatic are the projections for Latin America. Estimated figures show that by the year 2000 about 80% of the population of Latin America will be urban and that the figure will not be less than 50% for any country. (Portes, 1981)

Based on rates of increase in urban population throughout the world, Latin America seems to be taking the lead, especially regarding large metropolitan areas. It is estimated that by the year 2000, close to one quarter of the world's population will inhabit cities of more than 500,000 people; of these 1.5 billion persons, 300 million will be in Latin America. 47% of Latin American population may be living in these cities of more than 500,000 inhabitants, and this would be almost twice the ratio for the world as a whole. Some 1978 United Nations projections for the year 2000 indicated that Mexico City and São Paulo will be the two largest cities in the world with populations of 30,000,000 and 25,800,000 respectively, and although these now seem to be overestimates, they may not be that far off the mark as metropolitan region projections. Although demographic data are often subject to revision, and future projections are based on current assumptions, the statistics presented above demonstrate the magnitude of urbanization in the Western Hemisphere.

The problems of urbanization have impressed themselves on the public in many forms. At times, the city becomes an arena for social problems, like poverty or the tensions of growth, which are national in origin. At other times, the problems are more specifically engendered by urban living: issues of housing, crowding, finance of government services, and local political participation, for example.

In the United States, crowding, transport, housing, assimilation of minorities, political participation and the avoidance of corruption have long been recognized as urban concerns. But in the 1960s, a perceived urban crisis occurred, as part of the nation's larger struggles over minority civil rights. Urban unrest focused demands for jobs, political enfranchisement, and integration or community control.

In the 1970s, these concerns were superseded in part by a new set of problems. The "fiscal crisis" of major cities focused attention on funding of services, their distribution and the efficiency of their provision, along with issues of job loss and "deindustrialization." The same concerns were later projected to the national level in the 1980s debates over national budgets and "Reaganomics."

In Latin America, urban problems were initially seen as quite distinct from those of the United States. Rapidity of urban growth, rather than decline, was the order of the day. Poverty and marginalization, basic deficiencies in public services and housing, and the need to slow urban growth through birth control or population diversion (to smaller cities or back to the land) were the principal focus of attention throughout the period of the Alliance for Progress and on into the 1970s.

The demographic and service problems have not abated, but in the 1980s Latin American cities have also come to suffer from North American-style urban problems. The debt crisis parallels in some ways the earlier fiscal crisis of the north. Even more striking is the sudden emergence of new demands for popular participation, and a newfound importance of the roles of mayors and urban state governors, that parallels some of the North American concerns of the 1960s.

Urban research in the past has rarely grouped the Western Hemisphere countries as a unit for study. United States cities are usually compared to each other or studied in relation to those of Great Britain and other industrialized nations. Latin American cities are studied by country or as a group, and they are sometimes compared to Asian and African cities. (For an exception see Wirth and Jones, 1978.) Historically the United States has tended to be oriented more toward Europe in its social and political relationships.

Despite occasional statements about commonality, comparative work has been focused on differences, with a presumption that urbanization is different in the two Americas. The literature of Latin American urbanization, whether inspired by the modernization school or the dependency school, saw cities as fundamentally different from their more modern or less dependent North Atlantic counterparts. This differentiation was exaggerated by the tendency to focus primarily on points of major difference. For example, during the 1970s more work was done on such "informal" sectors as squatter housing, and marginal craft and commercial businesses, than on formal housing, employment and business. For summaries of this literature see Roberts (1976), Gilbert and Gugler (1982), Portes and Walton (1976, 1981), Armstrong and McGhee (1985). Many of these studies were excellent, but certain areas, such as the role of mayors, were left unstudied. Theoretical understanding could also be muddied: when some degree of informality turned up in studies of the North American "underground economy," this was presumed to be a result of underdevelopment rearing its head, rather than a sign that certain similarities occur between urban areas at different points in the world system. One of our principal conclusions is that a simple dichotomization of cities by national level of development is misleading. (C.f. Edel, 1988)

IV
Some Conclusions and Directions for Research

Within the comparative focus suggested here, our work points to some preliminary conclusions and directions for research. In our initial proposal we had suggested that the urban challenge in the hemisphere could be identified initially in demographic terms. Our seminar experience, however, suggests the issue is not merely one of numbers, although the demographic problems are certainly severe. Additional elements not as initially apparent include economic interdependence, and the simultaneity of increasing financial crises.

Increasing Economic Interdependence
This has led to considerable economic opportunities for Latin America to develop exports, particularly in new industrial areas, but it has often led also to restrictions on the power of individual governments to act to resolve domestic problems. Raymond Vernon (1971) suggested nearly two decades ago that the growth of multinational corporations might restrict the state's power to act. The past decade suggests that closer financial and trade relationships create such limits, even apart from the presence of multinational corporations per se. (Indeed, the importance of multinationals has sometimes been exaggerated; policy options in the Dominican Republic, for example, are more constrained by international debt today than they were by the presence, imposing though it was, of Gulf and Western a decade ago).

The effects of trade, finance and the like may seem to be national or international problems, rather than urban or metropolitan problems. But we argue that the new situation does focus our attention on cities in several ways. First, metropolitan growth is frequently accelerated by the new international division of labor, as Hymer (1972) pointed out. The link occurs both through the office activities that Hymer cited, and through manufacturing investment. It also occurs through the expulsion of peasants from rural areas as export agriculture expands. (cf. Armstrong and McGhee 1985).

Second, the new situation creates direct interdependencies between cities. This is most easily seen in the border-city relationships of Tijuana and San Diego, or El Paso and Ciudad Juárez, where the municipal services of one city are used by residents of the other. But it occurs as well through longer distance relationships. The migration relationship between New York and Santo Domingo or some of the other Caribbean cities is almost as intense as that of Mexican-US border cities. Industrial integration involves complex patterns of outsourcing and other trade by New York's manufacturing firms. The quality of education in the Caribbean islands, or in mainland South America, affects the quality of New York's labor force. Labor relations and possibilities for municipal taxation are affected by their counterparts to the south. The degree of enforcement of drug laws in Medellín or La Paz directly interlinks with the problems of similar enforcement in New York.

Third, the decreasing autonomy of the nation state itself should be studied in the light of urban history. It seems to parallel a late 19th century loss of autonomy by municipal authorities, as economies became more national in scope. The experience of how New York, Buenos Aires and other cities came to live with that situation, and to become innovators in areas of social policy despite their lack of independent economic and administrative power, is an important lesson and precedent for today's nation states to ponder. In addition, the transfer of some powers from the nation state to the international arena may, paradoxically, require that other functions and powers be assumed at local or other subnational levels, just as the increasing national concentration of powers in the U.S. since World War II has led to new stimuli for submunicipal "community" roles in government.

Economic Crisis and the Impact of Austerity

One result of interdependence has been that virtually all of Latin America has been faced by a simultaneous economic crisis. In the past, even to some extent in the 1930s Depression, different countries faced their most severe difficulties at different times, depending in large measure on what their principal exports were, and on different possibilities of import substitution. The greater simultaneity of the present crises mean that migration or aid within Latin America, or subregional cooperation in trade, are more difficult as means to a solution. The similar (but weaker) financial crisis of New York City, and the economic recessions of the past fifteen years in the United States, are related phenomena, but they had their impact sooner. Inasmuch as New York City has had its service-financial sector rebound strongly, the New York recovery and the financial programs that led to it might be relevant as a model for Latin American recovery plans. However, the widespread nature of the Latin American crisis means that the developed areas must perforce share some of the costs of Latin American adjustment through migration and also through adjustment costs that may eventually be imposed on their banking system and export sectors.

In many of the Urban Challenge presentations, considerable attention was paid to the impact and form of the austerity imposed on Latin America by the recession of the early 1980s, the debt crisis and the specific retrenchments agreed to by national governments as a condition for IMF or private credit rollovers. Although the severe effects of austerity will be felt throughout the societies, the problem will be manifested heavily in urban areas, especially as the impoverished countryside continues to spew people into the cities. Mayor Peña Gómez made reference to food shortages and paralyzing riots in the streets of Santo Domingo. The impact on employment and industry was central in the discussion of São Paulo; that on housing and poverty in the discussion of Mexico. In Brazil and Argentina austerity is a major complicating factor in the democratization process. In all cases, the economic belt-tightening complicates the orderly functioning of municipal finance and makes more difficult the ongoing problems of coping with rapid urban population growth and the coordination of city and surrounding-area governmental units.

Many colloquium participants had also done previous work on the New York City crisis and on subsequent state and national austerity measures in the United States. It has been possible to draw certain parallels both in terms of causes and institutional consequences. It appears that all these crises are part of a worldwide period of broader economic problems accompanied by economic and financial readjustments. The period since the early 1970s has been marked by rapid swings in commodity and loan markets. A tendency to loan overextension, and to subsequent bankruptcies or debt/fiscal crises, has been endemic in the international system. The fact that New York's fiscal crisis came early in the process makes the New York case especially valuable and important for study.

Austerity will not only change the economic and physical conditions in cities; it will impact as well on Latin American urban cultures. Migration of rural people to urban areas creates changes in expectations, ways of life, settlement patterns, social networks, work patterns and political participation. As a country's urbanites begin to outnumber their rural counterparts, the social fabric of an entire nation is modified. Cultural patterns of cities change not only with increased migration from outside but also with increasing conditions of austerity within the city. In her colloquium presentation on Buenos Aires, Elizabeth Jelin spoke of declining access to public goods under the military regime in Argentina and how this altered people's sense of self and dignity. These cutbacks also led to other problems such as insecure incomes and unsafe streets. A comparison between Buenos Aires and New York City was made by John Mollenkopf, who pointed to the decline and then gentrification of the central city, the geographic shuffling of poverty, the public goods and the rise of private consumerism.

Mayor Peña Gómez addressed the problems of "precarious human settlements" in Santo Domingo and other Latin American cities. A lack of fundamental services, rising prices and the general weakness of authority may lead cities to become centers of armed violence. Dr. Abad Gómez was particularly concerned about the medical consequences of violence in Medellín, Colombia, which he believed to be a symptom of profound social disorders caused by growing economic problems.

In Mexico City, similar problems of housing, lack of urban services, falling real incomes and proliferating environmental hazards also lead to growing resentment and anger, protests and rising political unrest. Both Mayor Peña Gómez and Dr. Abad Gómez suggested the resulting cultural disruption could spread to New York via migration.

All of these situations and circumstances affect attitudes, social structure and culture. They have an impact on male/female relationships, the family, the workplace, social networks and intraregional integration. As the Latin American urban dwellers become migrants to U.S. cities, the social fabric of these latter cities changes as well. Those escaping a life characterized by the descriptions presented above bring with them preconceived notions of life, work and social structure, much of which is based on their necessity to overcome hardships, survive and create improved circumstances for future generations. In addition, these, as other groups of immigrants in the past, bring along their cultural baggage, language, styles, art, music, food and traditions, which become a part of the U.S. cities in which they resettle.

Urban Leadership

Another factor in need of study is the formal institutional and political leadership of metropolitan areas. In the past two decades this has been an area of great neglect in the literature of Latin American studies, while attention has focused on broad structural trends in the international system, or on the informal sector at the local level. Under either emphasis, the roles of mayors and other city officials, of administrative agencies, of citywide business or citizens organizations and the like have been overlooked. Indeed, reading the literature on Latin American cities published recently, one would learn a good deal about grassroots leaders in poor neighborhoods, but virtually nothing about the city and business officials with whom they must try to deal.

This neglect needs redress. The Urban Challenge colloquia suggested that the role of mayor is being re-politicized within Latin America. In Brazil, campaigns for the mayorality of São Paulo and the governorship of Rio de Janeiro have been crucial indicators of party position within the democratization process. In Mexico, mayoral and gubernatorial contests in the north constituted the first major challenge to the ruling PRI in decades, while post-earthquake Mexico City has seen new debates over popular participation in governance. Argentina's democratization has opened a debate on relocating the national capital from Buenos Aires to the south. Colombia has adopted a reform that makes mayors elected, not appointed, while a former (appointed) mayor of Bogotá, Virgilio Barco, has become President. Mayors of Lima and Santo Domingo have run spirited, if unsuccessful, presidential campaigns from the Left. In Cuba, the creation of "local power" positions provided the only electoral element in an otherwise appointive political system. And in the small towns of El Salvador,

Peru and several other countries, local mayors' lives are literally on the line in civil wars. That role, and that of other sectors of local government, and of national governments, local agencies need to be studied.

Local leadership can, of course, come from outside of government as well. The one area of urban politics that has been studied closely in recent years has been the mobilization of low income residents. But other private groups need to be considered as well. As our colloquia demonstrated in the case of Medellín, the local business sector has played an important role in urban development policy. In Santo Domingo, the mayor has been developing public-private partnership efforts. Until the mid-1960s, studies of the traditional leadership of smaller Latin American cities, or of the leadership during formative years of the present megacities, often focused on the role of local private elites. But lately studies of local leadership from the private sector have been as scarce as studies of city officials.

A major concern for local leaders throughout Latin America is the issue of city-suburb coordination. Colloquia speakers on Medellín and Mexico City discussed the problem even while focusing on specific program areas of health and housing. More direct discussion of the issue emerged in sessions on São Paulo and on Buenos Aires, where efforts to develop new coordinating bodies was reported. The issue of metropolitan government in several Third World areas, including metropolitan Lima, was the subject of a comparative study by the Institute of Public Administration about fifteen years ago, but the topic has not been adequately examined since then.

Institutional Transferability as a Two Way Street

One of the aims of The Urban Challenge project has been to look to specific Latin American experiences for lessons on the design of administrative institutions. These might involve a transfer of forms (or a warning not to transfer them) from Latin America to the United States, among Latin American countries, or from the U.S. to Latin America (the most traditional direction for transfer). Of the many subjects and institutions discussed in the sessions, a number seem to be particularly promising as areas in which the United States should consider Latin American lessons.

One area is local community participation in programs, particularly for low income areas. The transfer of community development techniques back and forth is certainly not new. In the 1960s, agencies such as the Peace Corps and VISTA were actively involved in transfer of techniques. But there are further lessons still to be transferred. For example, New York has begun doing more in recent years in the way of sweat equity and self-help programs in housing. Obviously the rehabilitation of older apartment homes is different in many ways from the building of homes in squatter settlements or directed self-help neighborhoods in Latin America, but the concept is not something completely new. In fact, some of the lessons of Latin America, in terms of needs for flexibility in design, of the dangers of excessive mortgage burden, and of the problems of cooperation where different participators' rights were not clearly stated at the outset, might have been useful in the design of programs here. There are also more positive cases that could be emulated. A good example of emulation, from the health area, was presented in the discussion of Medellín, where the transfer of community health volunteer/promoter programs, from Cuba to Chile to Colombia, was examined in one of our sessions. The transferability of some programs between very different national institutional systems proved possible and fruitful.

A second area where there are lessons that should be considered immediately in the United States is the tying of social programs to funds related to specific areas of employment. Special industry-specific "social security" funds have existed in some Latin American countries, and have had major roles in the provision of housing and medical services (Mesa Lago, 1978). This has led both to certain efficiencies, and to certain problems, particularly in situations where covered industries were cutting back employment. An examination of the Latin American experiences might be useful to New York in areas such as health program. Alternatives, including HMOs and others, that will be considered in this country as part of the attempt to contain health costs, have their Latin American analogues.

Other specific points of commonality, and chances for learning, might be cited. The main conclusion, however, is that there is a common challenge of urbanization in both regions. Both appear to have a need for careful, holistic appraisal of urban development policies. The words of Victor L. Urquidi apply to both Americas:

The problems of urbanization are, of course, worldwide... Although the lurid descriptions of the industrial towns of the nineteenth century are largely a matter of history, today's economic wealth in the more advanced nations has not led to socially satisfactory solutions. Almost measureless contrasts remain between the living and housing conditions of the families in the upper income brackets and those in the underprivileged layers. Recent and sudden realization of those differences is demanding a serious reappraisal of urban development policies, and the consideration not only of the internal problems of each city, but of interrelationships of urban centers among themselves and the ultimate meaning of urbanization for a nation as a whole. (Urquidi: 1975; pp. 340-341.)

References

Armstrong, Warwick and McGhee, T.G. *Theatres of Accumulation: Studies in Asian and Latin American Urbanization.* London: Methuen, 1985.

Butler, Edgar W. *The Urban Crisis: Problems and Prospects in America.* Santa Monica: Goodyear Publishing Co., 1977.

Hymer, Stephen. "The Multinational Corporation and the Law of Uneven Development" in J. Bhagwati, ed. *Economics and World Order*. New York: The Free Press. Pp. 113-140, 1972.

Edel, Matthew. "Latin American Cities: Recognizing Complexities," *Latin American Research Review*, XXIII: 1, Pp. 165-174, 1988.

Gilbert, Alan and Gugler, Joséf. *Cities, Poverty and Development*. Oxford: Oxford University Press, 1982.

Mesa Lago, Carmelo. *Social Security in Latin America*. Pittsburgh: University of Pittsburgh Press, 1978.

Portes, Alejandro. "Population, Urbanization, and Migration in the Americas: An Overview of Recent Trends." Working paper, Center for Advanced Studies in the Behavioral Sciences, Johns Hopkins University, 1981.

Portes, Alejandro and Walton, John. *Latin American Urbanization: The Urban Condition From Above and Below*. Austin: University of Texas Press, 1976.

—*Labor, Class and the International System*. New York: Academic Press, 1981.

Roberts, Bryan. *Cities of Peasants*. Beverly Hills: Sage, 1976.

Urquidi, Victor. "The Underdeveloped City," in Jorge E. Hardoy, ed. *Urbanization in Latin America*. New York: Doubleday, 1975.

Vernon, Raymond. *Sovereignty at Bay*. New York: Basic Books, 1971.

Wilkie, James W. and Haber, Stephen, co-editors. *Statistical Abstract of Latin America, Vol. 21*. Los Angeles: UCLA Latin American Center Publications, 1981.

Wirth, John D. and Jones, Robert L., eds. *São Paulo and Manchester: Problems of Rapid Urban Growth*. Stanford: Stanford University Press, 1978.

1 Metropolitan São Paulo: Problems and Perspectives

by Vilmar E. Faría

The Metropolitan Area of São Paulo (MASP) is one of the world's largest urban agglomerations, with a population of 13 million people. In 1982, the MASP had a per capita income of about US $4,000.00, one of the highest among Third World metropolitan areas. At the same time, however, almost 30% of its labor force was earning monthly salaries of less than US $2,000.00 a year, and in several of its poorest areas infant mortality rates were around 10%.

This paper offers a summary description of the development process of this huge Third World metropolitan region, as well as a brief picture of its present social and economic situation with regard to employment, income distribution, and urban and social public services. At the end of the paper an attempt is made to present a list of some measures that should be considered to deal with the urgent social, urban, and economic problems of metropolitan São Paulo.

As a preliminary attempt to cover a variety of complex questions, this paper will emphasize data presentation instead of developing an analytical framework for the MASP's problems. However, a general theoretical perspective derived from political economy and development sociology underlies the whole discussion and has been presented elsewhere. For comparative purposes, it is important to recognize that in the MASP, industrial production for the national market has reached significant levels of size and complexity. This metropolitan area of the world periphery is the geographic center of the Brazilian industrial economy. Brazil is the tenth world industrial power in terms of gross domestic industrial output, with production highly concentrated in the state of São Paulo. It is, therefore, the emergence and consolidation of one of the first modern industrial metropolitan areas of the Third World that we will be discussing here.

The author would like to thank Pedro Luiz Barros Silva, Eduardo Fagnani, Celso Lamparelli, Guido Lopez, and Sonia Maria Begueldo. Without their active help it would have been impossible to write this paper.

I
The Metropolitan Area of São Paulo:
Brief Historical Background

From an administrative point of view, the Metropolitan Area of São Paulo—legally created in 1969—comprises 37 autonomous municipalities (*municipios*) including the municipality of São Paulo. In this metropolitan agglomeration more than 12 million people were living in 1980 (12,719,072) in an area of 7,967 square kilometers. This represented almost 10% of the total Brazilian population, and nearly 20% of Brazil's urban people. Together with the Metropolitan Area of Rio de Janeiro, the MASP performs the functions of heading the Brazilian system of cities, organized in a complex hierarchy of more than 480 urban centers (defined as urban areas of 20,000 or more inhabitants) where more than 60 million persons were living in 1980.

The core of Brazil's modern urban-industrial activities is located in the MASP. In 1975, 45% of the total value added by the Brazilian manufacturers was generated there. Most of the country's more important business and communication services are concentrated there too, including the banking and financial sectors, the largest publicity agencies, two of the four national newspapers and the largest and most important Brazilian university.

The growth of the MASP, however, is a relatively recent one. Even though some of its municipalities are among the oldest of the country (the city of São Paulo, for instance, was founded in 1554), until the first half of the 19th century they performed only local functions. The city of São Paulo itself performed only regional central place functions until the end of the last century, since Rio de Janeiro was, indisputably, the national metropolis. In fact, by 1890, while Rio de Janeiro already had more than 500,000 inhabitants, the city of São Paulo barely surpassed the 60,000 figure.

The development, first of the city of São Paulo, and later on (after 1940) of the MASP as a whole, is the urban result of the development process which has been taking place in the last hundred years and comprises three main phases or cycles. The first was commanded by the expansion of the coffee export sector located in the state of São Paulo in the last decades of the 19th century and first decades of the 20th century. The city of São Paulo benefited from locational advantages as an import-export commercial center and, increasingly, as an industrial area supporting the expanding coffee economy. In this first period the area benefited from growing waves of European migrants who provided it with a diversified pool of human resources, from a growing network of communications with its hinterland, and from an important urban infrastructure.

The second phase, starting in the 1920s, was commanded by consumer-goods import-substitution industrialization. The city of São Paulo benefited from the proximity to the growing internal market created by the coffee economy. It also offered advantages in terms of hydro-electrical energy and good transportation connections with the hinterland. By 1940, the state of São Paulo surpassed Rio de Janeiro in terms of value added by manufacturing. The city of São Paulo got the lion's share of this industrial expansion.

After the Second World War, and particularly during and after the 1950s, a third cycle took place commanded by the expansion of the capital and durable consumer good sectors of industry. The growth process which has taken place in Brazil in the last thirty years has completely changed the structural outlook of the country. Data presented in Table 1 show the magnitude of these changes.

Table 1

**Brazil
Indicators of Structural Change
(1950 - 1980)**

	Indicators	Circa 1950 (%)	Circa 1980 (%)
A.	Urbanization		
	1. % living in cities of 20,000 or more	21.5	45.7
	2. % living in urban areas	36.2	67.7
	3. % of urban households	37.13	68.9
B.	Occupational Structure		
	1. Sectoral composition of the economically active population in %		
	a) Primary sector	59.90	29.93
	b) Secondary sector	14.18	24.37
	c) Transformation industry (Manufacturing)	9.40	15.66
	2. Occupations		
	a) % of primary occupations	57.81	(31.08)*
	b) % of technical and administrative occupations	10.34	(20.70)*
	c) % of industrial and construction occupations	12.64	(19.96)*
C.	Structure of the GNP		
	a) % from agriculture	24.9	13.2
	b) % from transformation industry	20.2	26.3
D.	Structure of the Industrial Product (Cr $1970)		
	a) % from non-durable consumer's goods	72.8	34.4
	b) % from durable consumer's goods	2.5	13.5
	c) % from capital goods	4.3	14.7
E.	Exports		
	a) Coffee	60.0	13.4
	b) Industrial Goods	-.-	56.6

Source: Faría, Vilmar E. "Desenvolvimento, Urbanizacao e Mudanças na Estrutura do Emprego: a experiencia brasileira dos ultimos trinta anos." In: Sorj, Bernardo & Almeida, Maria Herminia Tavares de, eds. *Sociedade e Política no Brasil pos-64.* São Paulo, Brasiliense, 1983, p. 118-163.

* = estimates.

The city of São Paulo and the urban area surrounding it have been the spatial focus of these changes and, as a consequence, the urbanization of the city first, and its metropolitanization later, gained momentum.

To analyze the demographic expression of this process of metropolitanization occurring after 1940 it is convenient to distinguish three sub-regions within the MASP: the core, formed by the municipality of São Paulo and two other municipalities adjacent to it; the inner periphery, formed by seventeen other municipalities surrounding the core; and the outer periphery of the MASP, formed by the remaining municipalities.

Until 1940, the process of urban growth was concentrated at the core region of the MASP. After that, as the data on Table 2 indicates, the rates of population growth started to accelerate first in the inner periphery and after 1960 also at the outer periphery. In the 1970-1980 decade the population at the core grew at an annual rate of 3.8%, the inner periphery at an annual rate of 6.6%, and the outer periphery at a rate of 5.9% yearly. As a result of these differential rates of growth, by 1980, about 72%, 24% and 4% of the MASP population were living respectively at the core, the inner and the outer periphery of the area.

Table 2

Metropolitan Area of São Paulo (MASP)
Population Growth (1940-1980)
Core and Periphery

Areas	1940		1950		1960	
	N	%	N	%	N	%
Core (3)	1,326,261	84.6	2,198,096	82.5	3,831,275	80.0
Inner Periphery (17)	151,635	9.7	345,696	13.0	808,066	16.9
Outer Periphery (17)	90,149	6.7	118,994	4.5	151,904	3.1
Total (37)	1,568,045	100.0	2,662,786	100.0	4,791,245	100.0

Areas	1970		1980		% a.a.			
	N	%	N	%	40/50	50/60	60/70	70/80
Core (3)	6,305,362	76.8	9,163,362	72.0	5.2	5.7	5.1	3.8
Inner Periphery (17)	1,637,929	20.0	3,090,471	24.3	8.6	8.9	7.3	6.6
Outer Periphery (17)	262,939	3.2	465,239	3.7	2.8	2.5	5.6	5.9
Total (37)	8,206,129	100.0	12,719,072	100.0	5.4	6.1	5.5	4.5

Source: Fundação de Instituto Brasileiro de Geografia e Estadística 1981 (FIBGE), Sinopse Preliminar do Censo Demografico

Migration from other regions, both from the state of São Paulo and from other parts of the country (particularly from the Northeast), has been the main source of metropolitan population growth. Even in the last decade, when the pre-existing population base was large enough to feed the growth process, internal in-migration contributed with 77.2% to the decennial population increment, although an important amount of out-migration also occurred (see Table 3).

Table 3

MASP—Components of Population Growth (Brasilian Censuses 1970 - 1980)

	N	%
Total	4,382,616	100.0
Natural (2.3% growth rate)	+2,095,233	47.8
In Migration	+3,838,701	77.2
Out Migration	-1,096,318	25.0

Data in Table 4 also indicate that by 1980, of the MASP inhabitants: a) almost 57% were in-migrants; b) 36.2% were in-migrants coming from other urban areas of the country; c) 26.9% had entered the MASP in the last decade, and d) 4.5% were in-migrants who arrived in the MASP in the last year of the 1970-1980 decade.

Table 4

MASP—Natives and Migrants (Brazilian Census 1980)

	A (City of São Paulo)		B (MASP)		A/B
	N	%	N	%	%
Total	7,114,258	100.0	12,588,745	100.0	56.5
Migrant					
Total	3,645,560	51.2	7,168,688	56.9	50.8
From Urban Areas	2,175,737	30.6	4,566,150	36.2	47.8
Less than 10 years	1,408,166	19.8	3,383,701	26.9	47.6
From outside the state	n. a.	-.-	1,919,736	15.2	-.-
Less than 1 year	205,888	2.9	562,249	4.5	36.6

Contribution of migrants to population growth in the last decade: 77.2%

This elastic supply of cheap labor for a long period of intense growth has been one of the main factors accounting for the two main characteristics of the MASP: a fast expansion of its urban base and the persistence of high levels of poverty together with the expansion of wealth. The rapidity of the industrial and service expansion of the MASP, based on an almost unlimited supply of cheap labor, has created a metropolitan area where the social contrasts are quite intense and the precariousness of its urban infrastructure is visible.

To focus on the growth and development that characterizes the MASP is only a superficial and one-sided way of referring to a large, modern, industrial, mass-consumption urban metropolis located at the world periphery. This growth has not solved the problems of widespread urban poverty. And an industrially-complex, urban, modern and poor society located at the periphery of the world system is a sociologically new phenomenon. A large amount of fresh research work has to be done in order to understand this new reality.

In what follows, a brief description of the MASP economic structure, income distribution and urban services situation is offered.

II
Economic Structure and Income Distribution

The economic base of the MASP is highly specialized in industrial and modern central place service functions, compared to Brazil as a whole. Data on employment, presented in Table 5, clearly demonstrates this.

Table 5

Occupied Persons by Economic Sector
Brazil, State of São Paulo, MASP, and São Paulo City
(1980)

	Brazil (a)		São Paulo State (b)		MASP (c)		São Paulo City (d)		c/a	c/d
	N	%	N	%	N	%	N	%		
Primary	13,109,415	29.9	1,175,002	11.5	41,418	0.8	8,204	0.3	0.3	3.5
Secondary	10,674,977	24.4		39.1		45.7		40.1		
Transformation	6,858,598	15.7	3,068,936	30.0	1,990,963	37.5	1,407,706	32.9	29.0	64.9
Construction	3,151,094	7.2	795,313	7.8	372,974	7.0	195,379	6.1	11.8	46.8
Other	665,285	1.5	134,193	1.3	62,266	1.2	36,563	1.1	9.3	46.4
Tertiary	20,012,371	45.7		49.4		53.5		59.6		
Distributive Services	8,065,601	18.4	2,027,625	19.8	1,184,625	22.3	776,436	24.4	14.7	58.4
Personal Services	16,089,709	16.2	1,946,814	19.0	1,104,618	20.8	745,728	23.4	15.6	56.7
Social Services	4,857,061	11.1	1,088,127	10.6	584,789	10.4	376,761	11.8	11.3	50.4
Total										
Total Population	121,150,753		24,881,001		12,489,407		8,444,460		10.3	50.2
Total Urban Population	61,253,666		17,605,147						20.4	70.9

The percentage of persons occupied in the secondary sector of the economy was 45.7% in the MASP, while the figures for Brazil as a whole and for the state of São Paulo were 24.4% and 39.1% respectively. Within the secondary sector it is the transformation industry (manufacturing) subsector which gets the lion's share: 37.5% of the MASP labor force compared to 15.7% for Brazil as a whole. In fact, almost 30% of the Brazilian industrial labor force is located in the MASP. The percentages of labor force participation in the distributive and personal services also reach higher levels in the MASP than for Brazil as a whole. Together, the "transformation industry," the "distributive" and "personal services" economic subsectors accounted, in 1980, for more than 80% of the MASP labor force, while this figure is slightly over 50% for the Brazilian labor force as a whole. The MASP is, therefore, the most industrialized area of the country and rough estimates indicate that its contribution to the total value added by the transformation industry in Brazil, by 1980, was around 40%.

An analysis of the internal structure of the MASP transformation industry shows a highly modern and diversified industrial sector. The capital goods and intermediate goods industrial subsectors contributed 77.2% of the total value added by the industrial sector in the MASP and more than 60% to the total industrial employment. The main industrial sectors are: the automobile industry, the metallurgical industry, the electrical industry, the mechanical industry, the textile industry, the food processing industry, and the chemical industry. Together they account for nearly 70% of the industrial employment in the metropolitan area (see Table 6).

Table 6

MASP—Value Added and Occupied Persons
by the Transformation Industry Sector (1975-1980)

	1975			1980	
	% V.A. Brazil	% V.A. MASP	% O.P. MASP	O.P. MASP	%
Automobile	71.8	13.8	11.3	214.998	12.6
Metallurgical	34.5	11.3	13.6	262.934	15.4
Electrical and Communications	70.0	8.9	8.5	168.514	9.9
Textile	42.1	8.9	12.7	135.349	7.9
Mechanical	54.6	8.7	8.7	160.927	9.4
Food Processing	28.8	5.3	5.2	76.263	4.5
Non-metallic minerals	32.8	4.3	5.9	59.912	3.5
Editorial	34.3	4.1	3.9	56.938	3.3
Chemical	35.4	8.1	3.7	80.951	4.7
Pharmaceutical	61.8	4.7	2.0	27.941	1.6
Garments and Shoes	42.5	3.2	6.0	103.168	6.0
Miscellaneous	61.8	2.9	4.0	61.626	3.6
Subtotal		83.4	85.5	1,409.521	82.4
Others subsectors		16.6	14.5	300.772	17.6
Total	44.4	100.00	100.00	1,710.293	100.00

As for the distributive and personal services subsectors, it is in the MASP where their modern branches are located (including the financial, information processing and research and development subsectors). However, it is important to emphasize that a large fraction of traditional and informal tertiary activities still survive in the MASP.

The economic development of the MASP in the last thirty years, although based on the expansion of a highly capital intensive industrial sector and upon the growth of a modern tertiary and quaternary economy, has not been able to produce a more equitable income distribution, or salaries for its working population commensurate with the gains in economic productivity. An elastic supply of labor and market regional and sectoral heterogeneity, and the persistence, for a long period, of an authoritarian regime that curtailed political and labor union mobilization and participation are some of the factors explaining the persistence of widespread poverty in the MASP.

The situation is severe, although it is better in the MASP than for Brazil as a whole. As the data on Table 7 indicate, in this most developed and industrialized region of the country, almost half of occupied persons (44.8%) earned less than two "minimum wages" monthly. The "minimum wage" is a statistical and legal figure, adjusted frequently for inflation. As of 1982, it was equal to $90 in U.S. currency. To have a rough idea of the purchasing power of this salary, it is sufficient to indicate that two "minimum wages" of monthly salary would barely permit the purchase of the minimum of food essential for a young family of three persons to survive.

Table 7

Monthly Income Classes of the Urban Labor Force (1982)
Brazil and MASP

Income Classes	State of			
	Brazil %	Southeast %	São Paulo %	MASP %
No income up to ½ MW*	15.8	11.9	8.1	
+ up to 1 MW	19.2	17.0	14.1	15.2
+ 1 up to 2 MW	28.3	28.6	29.1	29.6
+ 2 up to 5 MW	24.5	27.9	31.9	35.4
+ 5 up to 10 MW	7.8	9.2	10.9	19.7
+ 10 MW	4.4	5.3	5.8	
Total number	(33,681,851)	(18,373,543)	(9,899,853)	(5,534,185)

*1 Minimum Wage = US $90.00 of 1982

It is also important to note that, of course, economic activities and different income classes are both unevenly distributed throughout the several municipalities and subregions within each municipality. On the contrary, economic activities are highly segregated spatially, as are the different economic segments of the population. There is an intra-metropolitan territorial division of social labor: in some municipalities and districts within these municipalities—for better or for worse—there is a high concentration of modern and high productivity industries (some districts of the city of São Paulo and São Bernardo, for instance) while others are specialized in low productivity industrial and service endeavors, and still others which perform the function of labor force reproduction (municipalities and districts known as "dormitory cities," such as Barueri and Diadema).

This spatial segregation of classes of activities and income groups, resulting from the development process, is closely related to an array of urban problems (such as housing, transportation, and public services) facing the MASP. It is to these aspects that we now turn.

III
Growth and Poverty:
The Urban Problems Facing the MASP

This urban area has been growing at annual rates above 5% for more than fifty years. It has a population growth based on internal migration coming, to a large extent, from rural areas. The pattern of capital accumulation has been increasingly based on foreign multinational corporations (even if producing for the internal market). It has faced long periods of political demobilization and repression, and has a highly segregated pattern of spatial organization. The area has certainly accumulated, over the years, an astonishing number of urban problems. Most of them are linked to structural characteristics of the development pattern and to the persistence of widespread urban poverty. Others are linked to the nature of state power and the pattern of organization of public services, and still others to the nature of the relationship existing among different levels of government and to the distribution of governmental responsibilities.

In Table 8 a set of indicators is presented to offer a summary view of the main social and urban problems that the MASP was facing at the beginning of the 1980s.

Table 8

MASP—Main Deficits (circa 1982)

% of solid waste collected but not adequately treated	78.4%
% of persons living in households not served by the sewage system	64.0%
% of persons living in areas without solid waste collection	33.3%
% of households not served by treated water systems	17.0%
% of persons living in inadequate houses	10.6%
modal class of hours daily spent on urban transportation	3-4 hours
coefficient of infant mortality per thousand	55.0
% of persons of more than 10 years of age functionally illiterate	22.1%
% of employed persons not covered by Social Security	21.4%
% of families earning less than two MW	33.8%
% of persons holding irregular jobs	22.7%
% of open unemployment	10-15%

The immense size and the complexity of the problems underlying the indicators provided above are easy to grasp in terms both of social and economic problems as well as in terms of governability. Let us briefly analyze the most important ones.

Housing and Urban Infrastructure

Under the pressure of population growth as well as of the rapid increase in economic activities, urban expansion has been chaotic, particularly if we consider the economic and political influence of the interests linked to urban land development and to the construction industry. Together with the lack of adequate public programs for housing and urban infrastructure, especially for the poor population, these factors have produced an array of difficult urban problems. It is estimated that the housing deficit of the MASP is now around

300,000 households: there are about 500,000 persons living in shantytown slums (*favelas*) and about 1,000,000 people living in deteriorated multiple-family housing (*cortiços*).

Another aspect of the same problem is the large number of families living in areas that were opened for urban settlement without even the minimum legal requirements and urban infrastructure facilities. At the several urban peripheries existing around the MASP, there are several land developments (*loteamentos*) where the working class population built their inadequate houses by themselves, without having adequate property rights upon the land even though this land had been purchased and paid for at market prices. It is estimated that in the city of São Paulo alone there is an area of 311,474,774 square meters of land illegally occupied and developed!

The rapid, chaotic, illegal and highly segregated process of urban expansion put a severe burden upon the basic urban infrastructure, particularly upon sewage collection and treatment and urban transportation.

By 1980, only 36% of the population of the MASP was living in areas provided with sewage collection systems. The proportion of sewage collected that was receiving adequate treatment was itself negligible. Most of it flowed directly into rivers and other water reservoirs, without receiving any kind of treatment. As a consequence the two most important rivers, the Tiete and the Pinheiros rivers, are practically dead.

Historically, two factors have contributed to create difficult problems of urban transportation. First is the spatial segregation of activities and of housing by income groups. Most of the working class population has to travel daily across long distances to reach their place of work or of study. Second, the development model of the last thirty years has been strategically linked to the automobile industry. As a consequence, emphasis has been given to individual transportation to the detriment of collective mass transportation. For the latter, preference has been given to buses instead of mass transportation (subway and railway), at least until recently. (The city of São Paulo's subway system started to operate commercially in 1975.)

The result, as the data in Tables 9 and 10 indicate, has been that about 40% of the daily trips are made by individual cars and almost 90% by either cars or buses. The impact of this mode of urban transportation in terms of traffic congestion, cost and environmental pollution is easy to assess. Besides, moving around the MASP to work, to study, or even to do some shopping is a costly, dangerous, and time consuming endeavor: modally, a person spent between three and four hours daily in transport!

Finally, it is worth mentioning that despite the fact that about 60% of the fresh water used in the MASP comes from outside the region, the water supply system functions at satisfactory levels. The main problem here is the cost of service: it is not uncommon to have several households in a region served by the water supply system that are not connected to the system because the household budget does not allow for such an expenditure.

Table 9

MASP—Daily Trips by Type (1982)

Type	N*	%
Collective (subway, buses, railway)	11,800	61%
Individual (auto and cabs)	7,500	39%
Total	19,300	100%

*(thousands)

Table 10

MASP
Collective Transportation—Total No. of Daily Trips by Mode

Type	N	%
Bus	9,800	83%
Subway	1,180	10%
Railway	820	7%
Total	11,800	100%

Health and Education

Health and educational services in the MASP, in aggregate terms and as compared with these services for the country as a whole, are in better shape than the services previously analyzed. In terms of desirable international parameters, however, the situation still deserves close attention from the government.

In the area of health, even if the coefficient of infant mortality is 55 deaths per thousand at the MASP aggregate level, there still exist some areas within the MASP where this coefficient is well above 80 deaths per thousand infants born alive. The same unevenness occurs with the availability and the geographical distribution of hospital beds. By 1982 there were 55,558 hospital beds available in the MASP—about 4.5 per thousand inhabitants. They were, however, extremely ill distributed and in at least eight of the MASP's "municipalities" there was no hospital bed available.

In the area of basic education, about 90% of children aged five to fourteen were enrolled at school. The main problems in this area, once again, are linked to the situation of widespread poverty and deficient urban services: the schools available are unevenly distributed, forcing students to travel long distances to school. Once in school, mainly for reasons connected to household poverty, many students have difficulty in remaining there. The last available information indicates that for each 10 students entering the first grade only 4 would remain at school in the 8th grade. Many will leave school because of inadequate academic performances associated with malnutrition. One strategic way to keep students at school would be to provide food all the year around.

However, the main problem associated with the health and the educational services in the MASP regards the daily working of these services, as well as the wages received by the personnel working in these sectors. Most schools and health centers are ill-equipped and the personnel receive very low wages. As a result the quality of daily services is bad.

Water and Environmental Pollution

As we have seen, the proportion of sewage collected in the MASP that receives treatment is negligible. Most of it flows directly into the rivers and other water reservoirs of the region. Industrial and hospital wastes have been also discharged in the waters without treatment for many years. As a result the level of water pollution in the MASP is quite high. Its two main rivers are completely dead, presenting a situation similar to that of the Thames River in the fifties.

Air pollution is another serious problem. The topographical and meteorological situation of the MASP, particularly during the winter, is unfavorable to pollutant dispersion. Some data are given in Table 11, below, indicating the number of days per month when the quality of the air reaches undesirable levels. Air pollution control legislation is inadequate and, in any case, difficult to enforce. The main sources of air pollution are oil combustion from automobiles and buses (there are about 2.6 million vehicles in the MASP) and industries, as well as from open-air combustion of solid wastes.

Another source of environmental pollution at the MASP is related to the problem of solid wastes: about 9,000 tons are produced daily, of which hospitals' solid wastes represent about 100 tons, and industrial solid residues about 2,900 tons (of which 130 tons are highly lethal). Only a small proportion (about 10%) of the solid waste collected receives some kind of treatment. A large proportion remains in open-air deposits of different sizes and locations, some of them dangerously near to sources of water supply and most of them illegally located and completely uncontrolled by public authorities. The existing plans to improve the situation, if executed, would only postpone a part of the problem for three or four years.

Finally, it is important to mention another problem that from time to time affects different areas of the MASP: periodic flooding. Due to the absence of drainage systems, as well as to inadequate control of rivers crossing the region, some areas are periodically affected by inundations. The damage to property, particularly in areas housing the poor, can be quite extensive.

Some of these environmental problems are highly correlated spatially, and due to segregation patterns some areas of the MASP accumulate many of them.

It is difficult to estimate the amount of resources that could be necessary to solve this cumulative array of problems affecting the quality of life of the

Table 11

MASP—Air Pollution
Number of days of inadequate air quality

Months		Particulate Matter		Sulfur Oxides		Carbon Monoxide		Ozone	
		I*	B*	I	B	I	B	I	B
1981	July/	48	1	1		6	1	9	5
	August	74	7	2		3	1	7	5
	September	111	10	8		2		11	7
	October			1				4	5
	November	1		3		4		13	4
	December			3				3	2
1982	January	2							4
	February	5				2		2	
	March	1				1		3	
	April	2				1		2	
	May	38	1			8		2	2
	June	5				2		2	
	July	27	2	1		1		5	
	August	15	1			4		7	4
	September	18		2				5	3
	October	3				1		9	5
	November	1		3		1		12	5
	December			1		4		3	2
1983	January					11		5	5
	February	2		1		1		12	6
	March	21		2		13		7	5
	April					9		4	2
	May					15	1	4	1
	June	6				19			
Totals		280	23	27	0	108	3	135	68

*I = Inadequate quality   B = Bad Quality

MASP population and, particularly, its poorest segment. However, to give a rough idea of the magnitude of the problems, let me quote from a recent press conference given by the Mayor of the City of São Paulo:

"If, by some miracle, the prefecture would receive today the thirteen trillion cruzeiros necessary to eliminate, in a year, the city's deficit in infrastructure, housing and urban equipment, São Paulo would gain over 6000 kilometers of paved and lighted roads, 1000 kilometers of sewers, 4000 childcare centers and almost a million dwellings, along with hundreds of health centers, dozens of hospitals, plazas and playgrounds."

In other words, the City of São Paulo alone would need 12 times its present annual budget to face its present problems (about 30 billion dollars, or about a third of the Brazilian external debt).

IV
The Impact of the Recent Crisis

The situation of the Metropolitan Area of São Paulo, previously described, has been the structural result of several decades of self-sustained growth and development, during which only a few periods of stagnation and recession of short duration occurred.

As is well known, the present world crisis hit the Brazilian economy very deeply. The cumulative effects of the crisis, particularly after 1981, immersed the country in a recession that is entering its fourth consecutive year. The crisis has been affecting, particularly, some important segments of the industrial sector as well as the construction industry.

This is not the place to analyze the causes and characteristics of this recession. It is relevant, however, to point out that the MASP has been suffering severely with the crisis, since an important proportion of Brazilian manufacturing industry, as we have seen, is located in the MASP. The data presented in Table 12 give some indications of the magnitude of the industrial recession.

Table 12

MASP—Indicators of Economic Performance
1975 = 100*

Variables	1975	1976	1977	1978	1979	1980	1981	1982	1983	1984**
Total employment	98.4	103.0	107.7	109.8	113.9	117.2	118.5	105.5	100.7	95.1
Total hours paid	98.4	101.6	104.0	106.3	113.3	115.7	113.7	99.1	95.4	92.1
Hours worked in production	93.8	99.5	101.0	106.8	111.8	117.7	114.3	94.5	87.8	86.2
Consumption of electricity	95.2	102.4	106.4	117.3	129.9	141.9	143.7	132.3	141.6	157.5
Real wages	93.2	105.0	118.4	129.5	144.1	149.5	155.7	162.9	160.4	138.1
Real median salary	94.8	101.9	109.9	117.9	126.5	127.6	131.4	154.4	159.2	145.3
Total retail sales	87.0	101.1	105.1	110.7	117.7	128.5	127.7	115.1	108.1	116.6
Index of activity	91.9	101.3	105.0	113.5	122.9	132.1	132.1	117.4	115.5	121.7

Source: State of São Paulo: F.I.E.S.P.
* For the year as a whole. The data in the table refer to the month of January and February of each year.
** Estimated for February 1984

This slowing down of economic activities has been affecting the quality of life at the MASP in different but cumulative ways. To begin with, the rate of open unemployment, which in the last decades oscillated around 2% or 3% of the MASP labor force, reached almost 10% by the start of 1984, even by the underestimated official figure of Table 13.

Paralleling the rise of the open unemployment rate, there was also some regression in the formalization of labor relations, with an increase of informal economic activities located in marginal sectors of the urban economy. A rough indication of this phenomenon is the proportion of employed persons working without legal registration, one of the guarantees that workers have that they will be covered by the existing social legislation.

Table 13

MASP—Open Unemployment Rates

Economic Sectors	Rio de Janeiro			São Paulo		
	1976	1983	% change	1976	1983	% change
Personal Services	52.6	49.9	2.7	56.6	47.7	8.9
Construction	81.7	59.7	21.0	80.5	67.8	12.7
Commerce	84.7	75.1	8.6	81.8	78.6	3.2
Production Services	84.7	81.3	2.4	89.6	83.4	3.2
Other Activities	91.5	90.2	1.3	95.4	95.3	0.1
Transport and Communications	90.3	91.0	-0.7	91.9	90.8	1.1
Transformation Industry	90.6	82.8	7.8	94.4	91.7	2.7
Social Services	71.7	65.2	5.5	52.6	49.4	3.2
Other Industrial Activities	93.6	90.1	3.5	88.7	85.3	3.4
Total	73.8	66.4	5.4	82.9	74.9	8.0

Source: FIBGE National Surveys, 1976 and 1983
* Legally Registered
** Includes Primary Activities and Public Administration

Another consequence of the present crisis has been the acceleration of inflation, which reached 200% annually by mid 1984, with a correspondent impact upon the cost of living, particularly with regard to food and urban transportation prices. The first was aggravated by the agricultural policy, which subsidizes the production of sugar cane for alcohol production to counter the energy crisis and the production of export staples to face the balance of payments problems. The second was also aggravated by the oil crisis. The impact of these prices upon the lower segments of the MASP population is crucial: a high proportion of its household budgets is spent on food and transportation. The crisis hit most deeply those firms facing problems of financing as a result of the increase in the interest rates as well as those technologically less advanced. Once again this impact, given different locational industrial patterns prevailing in the MASP, has been spatially differentiated.

Finally, the decline of economic activities affected both the fiscal base of state and municipal governments and the performance of those public services whose income structure is based directly upon funds related to the pace of employment expansion. This was the case of housing, social security and health provision, in which key agencies nearly collapsed.

The growing unemployment, and the deep financial crisis of housing, social security and health programs in a situation of widespread structural urban poverty, put a severe burden upon the state and local governments and increased the amount of urban violence, the most tragic indicator of the depth of the present social crisis in the MASP.

Urban violence is an endemic phenomenon in an urban area with the size, complexity, heterogeneity and social inequality of the MASP. Although ethnically heterogeneous, and presenting a certain degree of ethnic spatial segregation, there is no visible violence along ethnic cleavages. Migrants of Italian,

Japanese, Portuguese, and Arab origin make a relatively peaceful living with Brazilians of both European and African background, despite the existing prejudices and discrimination. Urban violence in São Paulo, besides being related to several aspects of modern urban life, is anchored in the situation of widespread structural poverty. With the worsening of the socio-economic situation resulting from the recession previously described, urban violence has been increasing since 1981. This is particularly true of criminal offenses against property as the data in Table 14 indicate.

Table 14

MASP—Indicators of Urban Violence
1981/1983

		Crimes Against Persons				Crimes Against Property			
		Homicide		Assault		Burglary		Robbery	
Years		N	Change %	N	Change %	N	Change %	N	Change %
1981	Mun.	1,251		29,254		36,086		26,821	
	GSP	1,875		41,258		49,115		34,504	
1982	Mun.	1,275	1.9	29,762	1.7	36,127	0.1	24,680	-8.0
	GSP	1,820	-2.9	42,809	3.8	48,262	-1.7	30,439	-11.8
1983	Mun.	2,009	57.6	31,624	6.2	40,286	11.5	40,952	65.9
	GSP	2,837	55.9	46,639	8.9	56,198	16.4	51,987	70.8

Source: Secretaria da Segurança Publica/ Delegacia Geral de Polícia/ Equipe Técnica de Analise de Dados; Fundação Sistema Estadual de Analise de Dados - SEADE.
in: FEIGUIN, Dora. Criminalidade violenta e algumas hipoteses explicativas. São Paulo, 1984, mimeo.

Studies in this area indicate high longitudinal correlations between indicators of crimes against property and indicators of level of industrial employment (negative correlations of about .65) on one hand, and indicators of the cost of living for the working class (positive correlations of about .60). The MASP has also suffered, mostly at the beginning of 1983, from forms of social violence such as rioting, even if these could be attributed to the organizing efforts of certain political groups.

In summary, the recent crisis has been aggravating the social situation of the area. Despite some signs of economic recuperation, the MASP faces severe problems of unemployment, rising cost of living, and increasing urban violence.

There is, however, another face of this poverty and social crisis coin. It is also in the MASP that you have the most well organized and autonomous trade unions in Brazil (such as the metallurgical workers' union), a growing array of grass roots social movements, and an active and progressive "intelligencia." It is in São Paulo that two of the most important and modern political parties, the PMDB and the Partidos dos Trabalhadores, find their stronger active support, providing the country with a new leadership coming from several sectors of the society. The MASP has, therefore, an enormous potential for progressive change.

The Metropolitan Area of São Paulo can be characterized as an area polarized by the contrast between its impressive performance as an economic center, and the levels of poverty and inequality still prevailing. As a metropolitan area typical of the modern urban industrial mass consumption society, particularly for Third World standards, the MASP impresses by the modernity and complexity of its industrial base, by the strength of its financial institutions, by the differentiation of its commercial network, by the sophistication of some segments of its personal services subsectors, by the richness of its cultural life, and by its potential for sustained economic growth. As a metropolitan area of the World Periphery the MASP touches the humanitarian sensibility for the widespread poverty that contrasts with its richness: the sprawling of *favelas* and *cortiços*, the lack of adequate urban infrastructure, the pollution of its environment, the violence of its streets.

The situation in the MASP concerns us for the hugeness of its problems and for its growing ungovernability. By way of conclusion some of the measures that should be taken, at the macro-structural level, are summarily presented.

Conclusions:
Setting an Agenda for the Near Future

As can be seen, the Metropolitan Area of São Paulo presents a rather long list of difficult problems. Some of them are structural, others have been aggravated by the present crisis; some are linked to the Brazilian economic organization and its local expression, others derive from the existing political and administrative structure both at city and metropolitan levels; most are linked to the present fiscal structure which does not leave enough financial resources at the local, metropolitan and state government levels. Therefore, it is difficult to set an agenda of possible solutions. In the short term, however, it is urgent that some measures be considered.

First of all, it is necessary to take measures to put an end to the present recession and to stop inflation. If the Brazilian economy returns to its historical rates of economic growth, the present unemployment rates will decrease and the control of inflation will positively affect the cost of living problem. In order to put the economy back into a growth pattern, the country—and the international economic system—will have to find structural and long term solutions to the problem of the external debt, in terms both of long term rescheduling of payments and of inflow of new investments. According to Brazilian economists, a deep restructuring of the Brazilian financial system should also be urgently considered.

Second, it is important to reform the Brazilian fiscal system in terms of its tax structure, tax levels and distribution as well as in terms of control by the different levels of government. State and local levels of government should have control over larger portions of the fiscal income as well as an autonomous—but democratically controlled—and more flexible taxing capacity. These reforms would increase the financial resources of local authorities. More demo-cratic control would permit planning of local and state government expenditures taking the local demands of the citizenship into due consideration.

Third, it is necessary to change the prevailing structure of the public sector operating in the area of basic social services (particularly housing, public health, transportation, energy and water supply and environmental control). The agencies in charge of these sectors should be planned to operate efficiently, but oriented toward goals of social equality rather than toward goals of mar-ket-oriented economic success. This would increase the supply of public services for those who cannot pay market prices for them, and would benefit the poorest segments of the MASP population.

Fourth, a political, juridical and administrative reform should be consid-ered. The main objective of this reform should be a new organization of both mu-nicipal and metropolitan politico-administrative structure. At the municipal level different measures are needed to differentiate local powers according to size, economic base and function within the metropolitan division of labor. In-creasing executive decentralization and improving the existing mechanisms and creating new ones of popular control over public decisions is urgent. At the met-ropolitan level, coordinating authorities, supported by adequate amounts of fi-nancial resources, political power and juridical legitimacy, have to be created to deal with problems requiring metropolitan consideration.

Fifth, it is necessary to plan ahead, considering the technological innova-tions to come. There is some risk that industry-sectors located in the MASP may become obsolete in the near future. Without an adequate long term policy to at-tract new sectors and to facilitate the restructuring of the existing ones, there is a risk of economic decay and urban blight.

Finally, although quite obvious, it is important to emphasize that these measures are only possible if the process of democratization proceeds and takes deep roots in the near future.

2 Concentration or Deconcentration? Mexico City and its Region

by
Orlandina de Oliveira and Humberto Muñoz García

Translated from Spanish by
Henriette Goldstein

I
Introduction

Economic-demographic concentration[1] in Mexico City and the process of deconcentration are two much-discussed subjects in Mexico today. They have been important political preoccupations for a long time, as is evidenced by many plans and programs formulated by the government (Garza, 1983). Uneasiness about these matters gathered even more momentum after the September 1985 earthquake. Systematic studies to date help answer several questions and concretely establish a wider perspective of analysis with respect to the complex of problems of Mexico City and its metropolitan area (Bataillon, 1972; Garza, 1980, 1985a; CEDDU 1985).

In order to understand the problem of concentration in Mexico, it is essential to recall some of the recent and earlier historical record. The region which surrounds the capital of Mexico—known as the central-eastern region—includes the Federal District and the states of Hidalgo, Mexico, Morelos, Puebla, Querétaro and Tlaxcala (Bataillon, 1972; Bassols, 1983). For centuries, this region has been one of the most populated of the continent (Sánchez and Moreno, 1968). The concentration of population has been on the increase: in 1910, 18.9% of the urban population (15,000 inhabitants and over) of the country was concentrated in the central-eastern region; this figure grew to 33.1% in 1940 and to 44.4% in 1970 (El Colegio de México, 1970; Bassols, 1983).

Since the Aztec times, the City of Mexico has been one of the largest in the world, and the most relevant activity and economic dynamic in the country has concentrated there. Political power has also been centralized in Mexico City since the last quarter of the nineteenth century, subsequent to the Independence and after a period of intense conflicts and wars. In the twentieth century, particularly after the 1940s and more markedly since 1960, Mexico City has expanded considerably in the area of the Valley of Mexico, and has formed a wide metropolitan area by incorporating several municipalities of the State of Mexico (Unikel, Ruiz and Garza, 1976). At present, the built up area within the Metropolitan Area of Mexico City has more than 1000 square kilometers, of which close to 50% is in the State of Mexico. The Zone spreads south in the direction of the State of Morelos. In 1980, the Metropolitan Area of Mexico City was made up of the Federal District and twenty-one municipalities of the State of Mexico (Negrete et. al., 1985).

From the perspective of the regional urban system, this concentration in Mexico has resulted in the existence of a primary city which influences its immediate area (Browning, 1962; Unikel, Ruiz and Garza, 1976). The expansion of Mexico City, together with the populational and economic dynamic of the country in the decades of the 1960s and 1970s, has reinforced the development of several cities of the central region, a short distance away by highway from Mexico City. For the specialists on this subject, it is evident that the central-eastern region of the country is on the way to becoming an integrated urban system, whose links between its parts intensify day by day. Recent trends point in this direction: the possible creation of a new perimeter of concentration in the cities which belong to the subsystem of Mexico City (Cuernavaca, Pachuca, Puebla, Querétaro, Tlaxcala and Toluca). The metropolitan areas of Mexico City and Toluca already constitute a megalopolis (Garza, 1985b).

The central region takes on special relevance within the framework of a search for alternatives to economic and demographic deconcentration of Mexico City. Because of lower economic, social and political costs, the main deconcentration of the capital of the republic may fall on the cities that are within the subsystem of Mexico City. Garza (1980) warns that with respect to industry, this deconcentration would be a serious mistake. At the same time, however, he accepts the inevitability of the tendency to form a megalopolis which will "enormously accentuate the problems that come from the macrocephalous growth of the urban system of Mexico [City]" (Garza, 1980). With regard to education, health and financial services and public administration, there would have to be an analysis of the viability and convenience of deconcentrating them toward the cities which surround the capital, in many of which there has been a significant growth in manufacturing and in services.

In this article, we present a brief characterization of the central-eastern region, especially of its urban areas. Among the aspects which we will consider are economic dynamics, trends in population growth, and the dynamics of labor markets. This latter aspect we will examine based on the available census data regarding the sectoral transformation of the labor force in the metropolitan areas and in urban municipalities (50 thousand inhabitants and over) in the last decade. We have a set of data and analyses processed by the Center for Demographic Studies and Urban Development of El Colegio de México (CEDDU, 1985), which constitutes crucial material for this characterization. We are interested in illustrating the extent to which some trends of distribution of the labor force in Mexico City have been modified in the context of changes which have taken place in the central region.

The comparison of Mexico City with the main cities of the region will allow us to develop some hypotheses about possible changes in the intraregional division of work. The ultimate purpose is to reflect on the options and obstacles of decentralization toward the interior of the central-eastern region, or out of it. Changes in the dynamic of urban labor markets, as an instrument of deconcentration, take on special interest. The creation of sources of work outside the Metropolitan Area of Mexico City requires a policy of spatial redistribution of public and private investment in administration, health and education, and in the productive structure. The energizing of multiple markets of urban work in the central region may constitute a fundamental element of attraction of migratory flows, which are an important source of population growth in Mexico City.

II
Mexico City and the Central Region:
A Brief Characterization

Economic Concentration

The most recent studies about the process of industrialization in the Metropolitan Area of Mexico City have shown that the degree of concentration of the industry in this urban center increased very substantially between 1930 and 1970, a trend which Garza (1980) regards as "a veritable industrial concentration with almost one half of the national manufacturing production." As the axis of the accelerated process of industrialization of the country, this urban center strengthened its role as the principal market of national consumption, and attracted industries of consumer and capital goods. The initial tendency toward concentration was consolidated by investment into the urban infrastructure by the federal and capital city governments, thereby giving incentive to the industrial growth in the capital of the republic (Garza, 1985a). In order to give an idea of the magnitude, it is believed that in 1970 the urban area of Mexico City concentrated 46.5% of the total gross income of industry (Garza, 1980). According to the same author, the preliminary figures of the industrial census of 1980 show that the capital city reduced its relative importance in the national industry. This trend occurs together with the increase in economic importance of the central-eastern region (Garza, 1985a). In 1975, this region had concentrated 61.3% of the value of industrial production of the country (Bassols, 1983).

Analyses done by Ruiz (1985) allow us to emphasize that production in the central-eastern region quadrupled in the period from 1960 to 1975. This increase was not of the same magnitude in all the states. (In the State of Mexico it was approximately sixfold, while in the Federal District it did not reach fourfold.) According to Ruiz, the growth of industrial production was exponential in almost all the states (with the exception of Morelos and Puebla). Nevertheless, the Federal District and the State of Mexico continue to dominate production in the region. It is worthwhile to emphasize that the production of durable consumer goods, intermediary and capital goods has a larger share in Mexico City, while the production of disposable consumer goods is larger in the other cities of the central region (Ruiz, 1985).

Industry has not only concentrated spatially in the central region, but a process of centralization has taken place as well, which in this sector manifests itself through the creation of ever larger enterprises (Garza, 1985a). The latter process may be related to the increase in the number of firms in fields such as metal products and machinery, which is one with high representation in the industrial structure of Mexico City, Querétaro and Toluca, and which has developed at high rates.

In short, the consolidation of a concentrated and centralized industrial structure has been taking place through a dynamic in which enterprises in the municipalities contiguous to the Federal District, such as Tlalnepantla, Naucalpan, Ecatepéc and Cuautitlán have become increasingly important. This has established an industrial belt in the State of Mexico which is connected with one of the manufacturing areas adjoining the city of Toluca. Leading industries, such as automobile manufacturing, which have established themselves in this belt, have been involved in this dynamic. These enterprises have also established themselves in various state capitals in the regions that surround the capital of the country, thereby promoting the expansion of manufacturing in this area.

Together with the economic-populational concentration, a highly diversified regional economic structure has been created. By 1970, the productive structure in Mexico City was one of the most diversified in the country (Garza, 1980). According to 1975 data (Negrete, 1985) the cities of Mexico, Cuernavaca and Puebla have a high degree of industrial and services diversification. Toluca has a high industrial diversification; Querétaro, of services; and Mexico City has a greater commercial diversification than the other cities. It should be emphasized that the diversification of the whole group of cities is superior to that of each one of them taken separately (Negrete, 1985). The central-eastern region will continue to be, even more markedly, the most diversified within the national pattern.

Little is known about the characteristics of the other sectors of the economy which are concentrated in the Metropolitan Area of Mexico City, and in cities of the central region. Some studies have been made of Mexico City's service sector, which emphasize some of its characteristics: there is a diversity of activity which ranges from autonomous work to the large commercial and banking corporation. Modernization, technological penetration and large enterprises have appeared in services which are complementary to industry (e.g., financial services). Distinctly capitalistic enterprise is a reality in all the branches of the tertiary sector, which leads us to believe that in this sector too a process of centralization has taken place whose magnitude and characteristics are still unknown. We must also consider the weight which public administration and the services offered by the government in health and education have in this sector, whereby a more comprehensive picture of the services in the capital of the country is reached.

In the case of services and commerce, it should be emphasized that both show a high degree of concentration in Mexico City. A study (Garza, 1976) illustrates that the number of service enterprises there increased by more than 75% between 1960 and 1970, at a higher rate (5.8) than for the whole country (5.1). At the same time, the share in the national total increased in the same period. Likewise, the tendency was seen for commerce, to the point at which, in 1970, the capital had 30.8% of commercial businesses. Thus, at this last date, there was a clear tendency toward increase of the degree of concentration of services and business. It has been suggested that in 1970, banking and finances were among the branches of the economy with the largest concentration in the capital (Muñoz, 1975). This last study also illustrates the high degree of concentration of the health, education (particularly at the higher education level) and federal public administration sectors. In short, the development of the tertiary sector in the capital is an offshoot of the very functions of a primary city, which somehow appropriated the capability to provide a series of services (the most complex and expensive) for the national entirety, for its adjoining area of influence, and for its own needs. It is fundamental that studies be made of the productive structure pattern of the urban areas of the central-eastern region, and to reflect on the meaning of industrial relocation in relation to the infrastructure of services in the capital of the country and in the cities which make up the urban system of Mexico City.

Urban Growth and Migration

In demographic terms, the growth of the country's capital has been one of the most dramatic in the world. The Metropolitan Area of Mexico City went from approximately 3 million people in 1950 to 8.4 million in 1970 and 13.4 million in 1980. Its growth rate has been rapid, though at a decelerating rate: 4.9% between 1950-1960; 5.2% between 1960-1970; 4.7% between 1970-1980 (Unikel, Ruiz and Garza, 1976). The decrease notwithstanding, the growth rate is still high. At the end of the century, the built up area of Mexico City may have a population close to 30 million inhabitants (U.N., 1981). The city's share of the overall urban population of the country had been increasing until 1970. During the last decade, its share has gone down as a result of the rapid growth of other important cities in the country, such as Monterrey, Guadalajara, Puebla and the northern border towns (Unikel, Ruiz and Garza, 1976).

The process of metropolitanization[2] and urbanization of the central-eastern region has been rapid too: by 1980 it included six of the fifteen metropolitan areas of the country and another five cities larger than 50 thousand inhabitants. Querétaro was the metropolitan area experiencing the greatest growth between 1970 and 1980, followed by Tehuacán and the metropolitan areas of Toluca, Mexico City, Puebla and Cuernavaca. In terms of growth trends, the cities of Querétaro, Tehuacán, Tlaxcala, the Metropolitan Area of Toluca and Tulancingo were the ones which increased their rates between 1970 and 1980 as compared with the decade of 1960-1970. Among the ones which decelerated their

growth are, in order of importance of the decrease, the metropolitan areas of
Cuernavaca, Cuautla, Mexico City and Puebla, and the cities of Atlixco and Pachuca (data prepared by CEDDU, 1985, see Table 1). In connection with the pattern of twenty five metropolitan areas of the country during the last decade
(1970-1980), the most dynamic areas of the central region experienced a lower
growth rate than that of Coatzacoalcos and Jalapa in the eastern region, Monterrey in the northeast, San Luis Potosí and Zacatecas in the northern region.
The growth rates of some cities of 50 thousand inhabitants and over, located in
different regions of the country, were in some cases much more spectacular than
the ones recorded for the metropolitan areas, as happened in Querétaro in the
central region (data from CEDDU, 1985).

Table 1

Total, Natural and Migratory Growth Rates (1960-1970 and 1970-1980)
of the Population in the Central-Eastern Region:
Metropolitan Areas and Urban Areas of 50 Thousand Inhabitants and Over in 1980

| | 1960-1970 | | Growth Rates | 1970-1980 | | |
Metropolitan Areas	Total	Natural*	Migratory	Total	Natural*	Migratory
Mexico City	5.43	3.04	2.39	4.27	2.80	1.47
Cuautla	5.15	3.68	1.47	3.46	3.57	-0.11
Cuernavaca, Mor.	7.06	3.68	3.38	4.14	3.57	0.57
Puebla, Pue.	5.39	3.29	2.10	4.23	3.65	0.58
Tlaxcala, Tlax.	2.97	3.95	-0.98	3.29	3.74	-0.45
Toluca, Mex.	4.45	2.88	1.57	4.49	2.36	2.13
Cities of 50,000 inhabitants and over in 1980						
Atlixco, Pue.	3.31	3.29	0.02	2.32	3.65	-1.33
Pachuca, Hgo.	2.75	3.43	-0.68	2.68	3.52	-0.84
Querétaro, Qro.	5.46	3.97	1.49	6.46	3.53	2.93
Tehuacán, Pue.	4.22	3.29	0.93	5.11	3.65	1.46
Tulancingo, Hgo.	2.03	3.43	-0.40	3.94	3.52	0.42

*The rate of natural increase corresponds to the state to which the metropolitan area or city belongs.

Source: Vital statistics and population census, 1960, 1970, 1980. General Statistics Bureau, Department of
Industry and Commerce, Department of Planning and Budget. Data processed by the Center for
Demographic Studies and Urban Development, El Colegio de México, project Diagnosis of the system of
cities and decentralization in the central region of Mexico (CEDDU, 1985).

With respect to population growth due to migration, estimates for the last
decade show that it was important in Querétaro, Toluca, Mexico City and Tehuacán; in the metropolitan areas of Cuernavaca and Puebla it had a smaller
positive contribution; Cuautla, Tlaxcala, Pachuca and Atlixco had negative net
immigration (CEDDU, 1985). It is worthwhile to remember that internal migration has played a key role in the growth of the population of Mexico City,
particularly beginning with the 1940s, which was a period of great socioeco-
nomic and demographic transformation in the country. The relative importance
of migratory increase compared to natural increase (due to fertility and mortal-

ity) has varied with time. The migratory component was the prevailing factor during the 1940-1950 decade, but natural increase surpassed it in the following decades (Unikel, Ruiz and Garza, 1976).

This occurred because the migratory currents had a different intensity in the various periods; there was accelerating natural increase until 1970. The decrease in fertility which was recorded as of the mid-1970s, partly as a result of the population policy implemented in the country, will contribute in the 1980s to the reduction of the relative importance of natural development as compared with social development (Oliveira and García, 1984). Despite the relative reduction of migration in the growth of the city in the last decades, the absolute magnitude of the flows continued to be considerable. It is estimated that the city received 2.5 million migrants during the last decade, compared with 1.5 during the sixties (Unikel, Ruiz and Garza, 1976).

Recent estimates of net migratory balances for the entire country indicate that the main population flows during the 1970-1980 decade headed toward the states of the central zone and some states in the north of the Republic. The State of Mexico, followed by the Federal District and Morelos, received the largest volume of migrants in the decade, while Hidalgo and Tlaxcala had negative balances (Brambila, 1985). According to this author the immigration to the metropolitan areas of the central region showed the larger net positive balance in Mexico City, followed by Toluca.

The net female migratory balance was larger than the male in this period in the five metropolitan areas analyzed by the same author (Mexico City, Toluca, Cuernavaca, Cuautla and Tlaxcala). Analyses for previous periods already showed the clear preponderance of the female population in the migratory flows which headed toward the capital of the country. The 1970 data indicated a selectivity favorable to women in all age groups, but especially those between 10 and 19 years of age. It seems that in Mexico, just as in numerous other cities, female migration occurs at an earlier age than for the male (Goldani, 1977; Oliveira and García, 1984). Throughout the last decades, Mexico City has received considerable female migratory flows, especially from areas of peasant economy surrounding the capital. A fundamental factor has been the existence of work for females, especially in unskilled service labor such as domestic employment. The role played by migration as a strategy for survival of the regional peasant economy must also be borne in mind (Oliveira and García, 1984; Oliveira, 1984). Concerning the differentiation of migratory flows to the capital city according to age, the tendency in other cities and countries has been clearly toward a preponderance of adolescents and young adults among the migrant population, as compared to the urban-born (Goldani, 1977).

A recent analysis (Brambila, 1985) of the net migratory balances in the seven states of the central region shows that those with a more dynamic economic development, such as the States of Mexico, Morelos and Querétaro, are the ones which attract, on average, younger migrants than the other states. In the Federal District, the increase in population is the result of the migration of young females, while in the State of Mexico there is a greater equilibrium between the female and male migratory flow. As in the Federal District, the flow of female migration in the States of Mexico, Querétaro and Morelos is younger than the male. Hidalgo and Tlaxcala show negative balances, and Puebla shows a negative balance for the working age groups (Brambila, 1985).

Sectoral Distribution and its Recent Changes

The industrial dynamic of the country and its concentration in the Metropolitan Area of Mexico City were contributing factors enabling the manufacturing sector and its associated business service to fulfill an important role in absorption of labor from 1930 to 1970. An examination of the average annual rates of growth of the population in the labor force engaged in each sector of the Federal District lets us assert that the producer services and construction experienced the most important relative increases in labor from 1920 to 1950. In the two following decades, manufacturing occupied second place in the growth of the labor force next to producer services, which had the highest annual growth rate (Muñoz and Oliveira, 1976).

From 1950 to 1970, all sectors of the economy, with the exception of social services, experienced a decrease in the growth rate of the labor force in the Federal District (Muñoz and Oliveira, 1976). It is important to emphasize that the propensity toward decrease of the labor force even included manufacturing activities. The figures for 1970 suggest that the growth of manufacturing in the Federal District succeeded in adjusting its productive structure to a continuous gain in the employment of labor. In manufacturing, the most significant increases in active population in the Federal District took place in such industrial branches as chemical products, metal products, and machinery and miscellaneous industry (Muñoz and Oliveira, 1976). To get a comprehensive picture of the recent dynamism of the labor market in the capital, we must add to the Federal District the municipalities of the State of Mexico which are part of the Metropolitan Area of Mexico City. As already mentioned, during the 1950-1970 period the capital showed a remarkable physical growth toward the municipalities of the State of Mexico, in which an important part of the industrial and services infrastructure became concentrated (Unikel, Ruiz and Garza, 1976). This process of expansion was strengthened even further during the decade of 1970-1980 (Negrete, et. al., 1985).

An analysis of the labor market in the Metropolitan Area of Mexico City for the period 1970-1980 (Oliveira and García, 1986) shows that the sectoral transformations of the last decade cannot be determined with the same clarity as in the previous decades, because of deficiencies in the 1980 census information. The great number of people not classified by sector of activity constitutes a great obstacle to the study of recent trends in sectoral changes. Several authors have searched for different ways of adjusting the information, but the results are not very encouraging when an attempt is made to evaluate the magnitude of the changes that have occurred (see García, 1984 and 1986; Mummert, 1985; Rendon and Salas, 1985; Oliveira and García, 1986).

In a study in which sectoral changes between 1970 and 1980 were examined, the Federal District differs from the municipalities of the State of Mexico which compose the Metropolitan Area of Mexico City (Oliveira and García, 1986). The study was based on data adjusted according to the extreme hypothesis that at least three quarters of the labor force insufficiently specified belonged to the tertiary sector. In the results, the secondary stands out because it did not increase its percentage share, but continued to hold around 40% of the labor force of the Federal District and of the Metropolitan Area of Mexico City in the last decade. The tertiary, in turn, which in 1970 concentrated close to 57% of the labor force of the Metropolitan Area of Mexico City, lost active labor force in percentage share terms between 1970 and 1980. The behavior of the tertiary was entirely due to what happened in the Federal District, because in the municipalities of the State of Mexico which comprise the Metropolitan Area of Mexico City, the relative weight of that sector reached 57% of the labor force in 1980 (Oliveira and García, 1986).

It must be underscored that the decrease of the tertiary in the Federal District and its simultaneous increase in the municipalities of the Metropolitan Area of Mexico City is not surprising. This process could have been related to the growth of middle class residential zones which employ domestic services, such as Satellite City, to the establishment of banking branches, and to the expansion of restaurant chains, recreation activities and commercial centers in the north of Mexico City. Negrete (1985) believes that the decrease of the tertiary labor force in the Federal District may be due to the specialization and modernization of this sector, which is a process that raises the qualification requirements of labor and generates less employment. Both hypotheses are viable and complementary, but we cannot discard the possibility that despite the adjustments made in the tertiary, it continues to be underestimated in the Federal District.

The tendency toward reduction of the tertiary labor force and maintenance of the secondary in the Metropolitan Area of Mexico City should be analyzed within the framework of what is happening in the country and in the main cities of the central region. A study of the changes in the sectors of the labor force, utilizing 1970 and 1980 adjusted information, supports the position that the population in the agricultural labor force in the country fell markedly, while the secondary held up with very similar percentages, and the tertiary increased (García, 1986). An examination of the changes in the last decade in the sectors of municipalities with 50 thousand inhabitants and over, and in the metropolitan areas of the region, provides an approximation of the behavior of the secondary and tertiary in the region. We adjusted the 1980 census information presented by Negrete (1985) using two criteria: one, clearly in favor of the tertiary (i.e., 75% of the insufficiently specified are assigned to the tertiary, and 25% to the secondary), and the other favoring the secondary (60% of the insufficiently specified are assigned to the tertiary and 40% to the secondary).[3]

The data presented in Table 2 allows us to assert that in the last decade, the labor force devoted to the primary sector declined. The labor force in the tertiary, in turn, increased in percentage share terms in all the metropolitan areas and municipalities of the region with 50 thousand inhabitants and over, except the Metropolitan Area of Mexico City.

Table 2

Distribution of Population In the Labor Force
of the Central-Eastern Region
According to Sector of Activity:
Metropolitan Areas and Urban Municipalities
of 50 Thousand Inhabitants and Over In 1980

1970-1980

	1970 (1)	1970* (2)	1980 (3)	1980* (4)	1980** (5)	1980*** (6)
Metropolitan Areas						
Mexico City	100.0 (2,834,707)	100.0 (2,632,049)	100.0 (5,019,400)	100.0 (2,936,372)	100.0 (5,019,400)	100.0 (5,019,400)
Primary	4.5	3.5	5.7	8.4	5.7	5.7
Secondary	38.0	40.2	33.8	53.2	43.1	48.7
Tertiary	52.9	56.3	23.1	38.4	51.2	45.6
Not specified	4.6	-.-	37.4	-.-	-.-	-.-
Cuautla	100.0 (26,709)	100.0 (24,294)	100.0 (43,981)	100.0 (30,763)	100.0 (43,981)	100.0 (43,981)
Primary	36.6	40.2	20.2	28.9	20.2	20.2
Secondary	16.6	18.2	15.1	21.6	22.6	27.2
Tertiary	37.8	41.6	34.6	49.4	57.2	52.6
Not specified	9.0	-.-	30.1	-.-	-.-	-.-
Cuernavaca	100.0 (53,583)	100.0 (49,070)	100.0 (95,564)	100.0 (67,529)	100.0 (95,564)	100.0 (95,564)
Primary	12.8	13.9	6.1	8.6	6.1	6.1
Secondary	30.4	33.2	23.5	33.3	30.9	35.3
Tertiary	48.4	52.8	41.0	58.1	63.0	58.6
Not specified	-.-	-.-	29.3	-.-	-.-	-.-
Puebla	100.0 (194,706)	100.0 (183,551)	100.0 (346,143)	100.0 (262,754)	100.0 (346,143)	100.0 (346,143)
Primary	14.4	15.2	9.8	12.9	9.8	9.8
Secondary	36.0	38.2	29.0	38.2	35.0	38.6
Tertiary	43.9	46.6	37.1	48.9	55.2	51.6
Not specified	5.7	-.-	24.1	-.-	-.-	-.-
Tlaxcala	100.0 (14,008)	100.0 (13,118)	100.0 (22,856)	100.0 (16,785)	100.0 (22,856)	100.0 (22,856)
Primary	33.3	35.5	21.7	29.6	21.7	21.7
Secondary	29.8	32.1	24.4	30.5	29.0	33.0
Tertiary	31.2	32.4	29.4	40.0	49.3	45.3
Not specified	5.7	-.-	26.6	-.-	-.-	-.-

(continued...)

Table 2 (Part 2)

	1970 (1)	1970* (2)	1980 (3)	1980* (4)	1980** (5)	1980*** (6)
Toluca	100.0 (98,085)	100.0 (90,831)	100.0 (183,681)	100.0 (137,777)	100.0 (183,631)	100.0 (183,681)
Primary	25.1	27.1	14.3	19.1	14.3	14.3
Secondary	30.6	33.0	24.8	32.2	32.0	36.3
Tertiary	36.9	39.9	32.1	42.8	53.7	49.4
Not specified	7.4	-.-	28.8	-.-	-.-	-.-

Urban Municipalities

Atlixco	100.0 (19,564)	100.0 (18,682)	100.0 (28,858)	100.0 (22,617)	100.0 (28,858)	100.0 (28,858)
Primary	41.7	43.7	34.9	44.6	34.9	34.9
Secondary	23.9	25.1	15.8	20.2	21.2	24.5
Tertiary	29.9	31.2	27.6	35.3	43.9	40.6
Not specified	4.5	-.-	21.6	-.-	-.-	-.-
Pachuca	100.0 (24,490)	100.0 (23,086)	100.0 (46,612)	100.0 (29,626)	100.0 (46,612)	100.0 (46,612)
Primary	5.7	6.0	2.4	3.8	2.4	2.4
Secondary	34.8	37.0	20.6	32.3	29.7	35.1
Tertiary	53.7	57.0	40.6	63.8	67.9	62.5
Not specified	5.8	-.-	36.4	-.-	-.-	-.-
Querétaro	100.0 (44,715)	100.0 (41,237)	100.0 (90,788)	100.0 (70,540)	100.0 (90,788)	100.0 (90,788)
Primary	17.9	19.5	6.5	8.3	6.5	6.5
Secondary	32.6	35.3	32.9	42.3	38.4	41.8
Tertiary	41.7	45.2	38.3	49.4	55.1	51.7
Not specified	7.8	-.-	22.3	-.-	-.-	-.-
Tehuacán	100.0 (17,899)	100.0 (16,770)	100.0 (36,580)	100.0 (25,693)	100.0 (36,580)	100.0 (36,580)
Primary	27.8	29.7	14.0	19.9	14.0	14.0
Secondary	30.2	32.2	25.5	36.3	32.9	37.4
Tertiary	35.7	38.1	30.7	43.7	53.1	48.6
Not specified	6.3	-.-	29.8	-.-	-.-	-.-
Tulancingo	100.0 (11,663)	100.0 (10,812)	100.0 (23,354)	100.0 (15,252)	100.0 (23,354)	100.0 (23,354)
Primary	21.6	23.3	11.2	17.1	11.2	11.2
Secondary	27.4	29.6	21.8	33.3	30.4	35.6
Tertiary	43.7	47.1	32.4	49.6	58.4	53.2
Not specified	7.3	-.-	34.7	-.-	-.-	-.-

Sources: Ninth and Tenth Population and Housing Census, 1970, 1980, General Statistics Bureau, Department of Planning and Budget. Columns (1) and (3) were taken from Negrete (1985), Table VI-A6-cb; columns (2) and (4) from Negrete (1985), Tables VI-16 and VI-17; columns (5) and (6) were calculated based on absolute figures presented by Negrete (1985), Table VI-A6-c.a.

* Those "not specified" are not taken into consideration in this estimate.
** Those "not specified" are distributed between the secondary and tertiary sectors 25% and 75% respectively in this estimate.
*** Those "not specified" are distributed between the secondary and tertiary sectors 40% and 60% respectively in this estimate.

The evolution of the labor force of the secondary sector is not as clear. In some cities, the tendencies we found were erratic, and varied according to the type of data adjustment used. Therefore, we feel it appropriate to view the figures with caution and only to point out general traits. The relative weight of the secondary is maintained or increases slightly in the metropolitan areas in the cities of Mexico, Cuautla, Toluca, Tulancingo and in the municipalities of Querétaro and Tehuacán; and it is maintained or decreases in the metropolitan areas of Cuernavaca, Puebla, Tlaxcala and the municipalities of Pachuca and Atlixco.

The estimates presented allow us to maintain that in terms of labor force participation, the tertiary sector has experienced a greater increase than the secondary in the main cities of the central-eastern region, except for Mexico City, where the tertiary sector has decreased in relative terms and the secondary has stayed at very similar levels. The industrial structure of the capital of the Republic continues to incorporate labor in absolute and relative terms, despite the loss of importance of the value of its industrial production in the national industry total. That is, the economic deconcentration does not necessarily imply a deconcentration of the population. In the central region, the pattern of relative increase of the secondary labor force possibly has occurred only in Querétaro, which in the last decade has consolidated into an industrial center. Cuernavaca and Puebla lose importance, both with respect to growth of industrial production as well as in terms of the relative weight of the secondary labor force. Toluca holds its importance as an industrial center.

With respect to tertiary labor force, it is possible to talk about a deconcentration process away from Mexico City: a) the relative importance of tertiary labor force decreased in Mexico City (because of what happened in the Federal District), and it increased in the other metropolitan areas and cities of the central region; and b) the relative participation of the tertiary labor force of the Federal District decreased in the total of the central region (according to figures provided by Negrete, 1985). It remains to be seen whether this deconcentration of the population of the tertiary occurs together with a loss of importance of public and private investments in this sector. Possibly, three processes occur simultaneously: populational and economic deconcentration of the tertiary sector of Mexico City toward other cities of the central-eastern region; changes in the internal structure of the tertiary and in the forms of organization of work in the various service branches in the Federal District; and relocation of service activities in the metropolitan area. Furthermore, as pointed out by Negrete (1985), the regional tertiary labor force has decreased its relative participation in the respective national labor force.

In order to better understand this possible process of deconcentration of the tertiary, it will be necessary to study in depth the economic and populational structure of this sector. Studies about concentration in the Metropolitan Area of Mexico City and in the central region have focused on the analysis of industrial dynamics. It is necessary to analyze the growth of the tertiary and its organizational changes in Mexico City and in the other cities of the central region. It will also be indispensable to know which factors influence the expansion of different types of specific branches of services in each of the urban areas which form the central region.

III
Conclusions

We have presented in this text a brief economic and demographic characterization of the central-eastern region of the country, as well as a series of data about the dynamic of the labor markets. In this section, we will formulate several comprehensive hypotheses which have been suggested by the entirety of the information, for the purpose of thinking about some of the options available for the deconcentration of the capital of the country. We start from the understanding that the subject matter is a complex process, inasmuch as factors of a social, cultural and political nature, as well as economic, intervene. It is a process to which greater research effort must be devoted. Also, the problem must be set forth as an equation whose parts will include the current state of economic crisis and the reconstruction needed as a result of the 1985 earthquake. From this conjuncture, we offer some considerations about the analysis of trends which, as we saw, only go as far as 1980.

One suggested hypothesis has been that the economic and demographic structures maintain an inertia which favors the development of a metropolitan region between Mexico City and the metropolitan areas and large cities located in the central-eastern region. To the continuous territorial and populational expansion of the capital of the country has been joined the population growth of the other cities. This is to a certain extent driven by the migratory flows which break off from the same area, and from other areas of the country, and in part as a response to a dynamic situation of employment creation in the urban labor market of the region.

Furthermore, in the analysis of the 1970 to 1980 trends, it was pointed out that in Mexico City industry had a slight relative loss of economic importance, while at the same time it maintained the relative total of its contribution to employment. It was also noted that the tertiary showed a tendency to reduce its labor force in the capital of the country. The questions we now formulate are: Up to what point are these tendencies related to the industrial and services growth which took place in some cities of the central region? Can it be said that what has happened in the capital is the result of deconcentration?

If, in fact, there was a movement of enterprises which left the capital and stayed in the central area, then what has been happening is a deconcentration which concentrates industry in one region of the country, which tendency surely has been aggravated by the establishment of new businesses. Actually, it is necessary to do more research concerning the spatial mobility of industrial capital and, in the specific case of the region, to see whether or not there are divisions between head offices and branch offices within the area.

The idea of deconcentration of the capital in the interior of the central-eastern region takes on significance because it has been held that the economies of conglomeration no longer represent advantages to industries located in the capital of the country. Mexico City, however, continues to be the largest consumer market in the national pattern. Thus, we can assume that the economies of scale represented by the cities surrounding the capital have become more attractive, among other reasons, because of the short distance which separates them from Mexico City and because the labor provided by the migrations is cheaper in the interior of the republic than in the capital.

In short, the concentrated deconcentration hypothesis must be analyzed more carefully. If there were evidence in its favor, then there would be a break between the inertia of the structures and the incentives (e.g. the generation of industrial parks, corridors and ports) and recommendations (to deconcentrate toward the Gulf basin region) which are contained in government plans.

Besides, another question must be raised, taking the example of industry as a starting point: In what measure is economic deconcentration related to population deconcentration in Mexico City? It is necessary to examine in greater detail up to what point there can be a relation between the relocation of enterprises (e.g. industrial) and a reorganization of the economic activity which will maintain or raise manufacturing employment in the capital.

With respect to the tertiary sector, we assume that, initially, the requirements of some services demanded by industrialization were generated from the capital of the country toward the cities of the urban system of the center. In the 1970s, the tertiary infrastructure began to consolidate and diversify in such a way that the relative magnitude of labor increased in several cities of the capitals of the states which make up the area.

In fact it would be possible to suggest that from the 1960s on, and more particularly in the 1970s, national banking, established in the Federal District, began to cover a good part of the country's territory, just like the large commercial consortia. It would be necessary to add to this the expansion of the tourist infrastructure in cities like Querétaro, Puebla and Cuernavaca. Up to this point, it can be suggested that the physiognomy of the tertiary in the capital possibly has been shaped by the fact that it is the financial center of the country, and perhaps also by a concentration and centralization of capital in its enterprises projecting an oligopolistic form of organization. That type of organizational structure could have favored the presence of branches of tertiary enterprises from the capital in cities of the central area and in the rest of the country, to the extent that for these kinds of businesses it becomes more feasible to homogenize and integrate the space of urban economy. It remains to be known how some of the branches of the tertiary have evolved in the cities of the central region and which part of the growth corresponds to services with low level of capitalization and to the deconcentration of public administration.

Briefly, the hypothesis we suggest is that the deconcentration of industry and services of Mexico City toward the central region has not followed a parallel movement. The growth of the tertiary in the capitals of states, furthermore, will perhaps be generated at a faster pace than to date, as a response to the same impulse of industry and the growing urbanization. In the coming years, moreover, that tendency will have to become more pronounced as a result of the displacements of activities and functions of the public sector and perhaps of the pressures which will be exerted by a growing urban labor supply caused by the migratory currents.[4]

The conurbation of the central-eastern area implies a spreading out of the regional division of labor and the formation of a large scale labor market, which will integrate the economy, the population and the society of this part of the country to a greater degree. Also in this respect, an open question for the future is the role which will be played by the city of Querétaro as a liaison point between the metropolitan region of the central-eastern area and the area of El Bajío. This idea already suggested itself in the mid-1970s (Unikel, Ruiz and Garza, 1976) by virtue of the fact that at that time, the services and commerce of Querétaro were already connected, in part, to the agriculture of El Bajío, while its industry was directly linked to the capital of the country. Thus, as the urban subsystems of El Bajío and the central-east gain importance, Querétaro will be strengthened as a link between both of them.

Still to be learned is in what measure the metropolitan region and integration of the central region will alter regional inequalities. One line of reasoning indicates that the increase of economic and population concentration of the central-eastern area will have negative effects on the future development of the country. But we may also assume, conversely, that the expansion of an area like this one may give rise to new stimulii to growth while, as a great focus of development, it may radiate changes in the agrarian sector in the interior of the area; better complement the countryside with the city; promote new investments; and assist in the integration of the industrial and economic system in the national whole. Finally, it can be assumed that the regional disparities will not be modified exclusively by this metropolitan region, but also by the dynamic to be followed in the tendencies toward concentration in other large urban patterns, mainly Monterrey, Guadalajara, El Bajío, the northern border and the southeast region.

In order for the regional inequalities not to become aggravated in the second five-year period of the 1980s, the deconcentration of the capital of the country and the metropolitan region of the central-eastern area will have to respond to a new long-term development strategy, programmed in various stages, under an original conception of urban life in the country. Such a strategy will have to take into consideration the social, spatial, administrative and political reorganization of the Federal District and the establishment of new economic balances in the country and its consequent political repercussions in the scheme of power redistribution.

It will also have to define the mechanisms by which a greater capacity to obtain financial resources might be generated in order to contribute to the growth of the urban infrastructure of the cities. This will form the basis of the metropolitan region of the central-eastern area in such a way that it will be able to resist geographic mobility, mobilization and changes of the social groups which will be affected by the comprehensive deconcentration process. This, in turn, entails a reinforcement of the civic organization, and that political institutions be renovated so that such changes will strengthen the country and be effective pivots.

Underlying the aforesaid is the connection between the economic and populational deconcentration process and the decentralization of power. The efforts required by a spatial reordering of the economy and the population cannot bear fruit except within a setting of effective participation by the citizenry, that is, in a context of greater democracy of the economic, social and political life. Power will have to be yielded to different public, state and municipal organisms and to different groups of civil society if, indeed, there is a will to decentralize and deconcentrate.

The agitation which the civilian society is experiencing as a result of the September 1985 earthquakes is proof that the great national tasks now require an active participation of the different organized sectors of the population. It will be difficult to achieve spatial economic deconcentration outside of a thoroughgoing societal reorganization.

The events of an increasing concentration have been associated with the acquiescence of urban societies to high degrees of social inequality, societies where social mobility and marginalization of broad social sectors have coexisted; it must be recalled that the intense industrial growth was based on long periods of declining salaries. The question then arises: to deconcentrate for whose benefit? To deconcentrate in order to increase profits, or to look for a greater participation of the popular classes in the benefits of development? There are many historical instances which illustrate how benefits are appropriated privately, while losses are socialized. Decentralization and deconcentration are priorities which must modify the country's model for development. A model to come out of the crisis will become real only if it is capable of conceiving and directing the mobilization of society and, therefore, if it has something to offer to the great majorities.

Notes

1. In this article, we use the term concentration and differentiate it from centralization. In the literature, a distinction is made between both concepts. In Marx, for example, the idea of centralization refers to the process which conglomerates many small capitals in order to form a few large capitals. Concentration refers to the major or minor accumulation of means of production of an individual capitalist with which he augments his demand for labor. More recently, the idea of centralization has referred to social urban processes, by which different spatial units are integrated in a territory and organized in a

hierarchical manner. In this sense, underlying this concept is the idea of power and its distribution. Spatial concentration, in turn, is a tendency by which economic activity and population conglomerate in a given space. Thus, centralization and concentration are two processes which are theoretically associated. In a given historical context, one can give rise to the other and they may mutually reinforce each other, although not necessarily.

2. There is an analysis in which the boundaries of the metropolitan areas of the country in 1980 are marked. In this study, 24 metropolitan areas were found, in addition to the urban region of El Bajio. The study includes the growth of the population between 1960 and 1980. (See Negrete, et. al. 1985.)

3. We deem these adjustments adequate for the urban areas, because of the lesser weight relative to the agricultural population. In the states with an agricultural population above 50%, they could lead to an over-valuation of the tertiary or secondary, according to the criteria used. We did the adjustment in favor of the tertiary in another study (Oliveira and García, 1986).

4. Note that the data which has been used does not allow the observation of the way the changes in the dynamic of the economy of the capital have had an impact on the sectoral transformation which occurred in the rest of the urban system of the central-eastern area until 1980. It follows, therefore, that more detailed economic studies are necessary at the level of sectors, branches and businesses, in order to be able to make a more precise evaluation of the process of deconcentration and its significance for the spatial division of labor in the central-eastern area.

References

Bassols, A. *México: Formación de regiones económicas.* México, UNAM, 1983.

Bataillon, C. *La ciudad y el campo en el México central.* México, Siglo XXI Eds, 1972.

Brambila, C. "Migración y crecimiento demográfico en la región centro," in Diagnóstico del sistema de ciudades y descentralización en la región centro de México. CEDDU, El Colegio de México, (mimeo), 1985.

Browning, H. "The Urbanization of Mexico." Berkeley, University of California, Ph.D. Thesis, 1962.

CEDDU. "Diagnóstico del sistema de ciudades y descentralización en la región centro de México." México, El Colegio de México, (mimeo), 1985.

El Colegio De México. *Dinámica de la población de México.* México, 1970.

García, B. "Dinámica ocupacional rural y urbana en el sureste de México: 1970-1980," *Demografía y Economía.* México, El Colegio de México, Vol. XVIII, Num. 3, 1984.

—"Desarrollo económico y venta de fuerza de trabajo en México, 1950-1980." CEDDU, El Colegio de México, (mimeo), 1986.

Garza, G. "Estructura y dinámica económica en la ciudad de México." Centro de Estudios Económicos y Demográficos, El Colegio de México, Thesis, 1976.

Garza, G. *Industrialización de las principales ciudades de México.* México, El Colegio de México, 1980.

—"Desarrollo económico, urbanización y políticas urbanas regionales en México (1980-1982)." *Demografía y Economía.* México, El Colegio de México, Vol. XVII, Num. 1, 1983.

—*El proceso de industrialización en la ciudad de México, 1821-1970.* México, El Colegio de México, 1985(a).

—"Dinámica industrial y perspectivas de descentralización," *Diálogos.* México, El Colegio de México, Vol. 21, Num. 11, 1985.

Goldani, A. "Impacto de los inmigrantes sobre la estructura y el crecimiento del Area Metropolitana," In Muñoz, H., Orlandina de Oliveira and C. Stern *Migración y desigualdad social en la ciudad de México.* Ciudad de México, México, Instituto de Investigaciones Sociales de la UNAM, El Colegio de México, 1977.

Mummert, G. "Cambios en la población económica activa de la región Centro Occidente, 1970-1980." CEDDU, El Colegio de México, (mimeo), 1985.

Muñoz, H. "Occupational and Earnings Inequalities in Mexico City. A Sectoral Analysis of the Labor Force." Austin, The University of Texas, Ph.D. Thesis, 1975.

—"Algunas contribuciones empíricas y reflexiones sobre el estudio del sector terciario," *Revista Ciencia.* México, Academia de la Investigación Científica, Vol. 36, Num. 1, 1985.

Muñoz, H. and Oliveira, 0. "Migración, oportunidades de empleo y diferencias de ingreso en la Ciudad de México," *Revista Mexicana de Sociología.* México, Instituto de Investigaciones Sociales de la UNAM, Vol. XXXVIII, Num. 1, 1976.

Negrete, M.E. et al. "Actividad económica y estructura ocupacional en la región Centro de México," in *Diagnóstico del sistema de ciudades y descentralización en la región Centro de México.* CEDDU, El Colegio de México, (mimeo), 1985.

Oliveira, O. "Migración femenina, organización familiar y mercados laborales en México," *Comercio Exterior.* México, Vol. 34, Num. 7, 1984.

Oliveira, O. y García, B. "Migración a grandes ciudades del tercer mundo: algunas implicaciónes sociodemográficas," *Estudios Sociologicos.* México, El Colegio de México, Vol. 2, Num. 4, 1984.

—*El mercado de trabajo en la Ciudad de México.* CES, CEDDU, El Colegio de México, (mimeo), 1986.

Rendón, T. and Salas, C. "La ocupación en México (1895-1980)." México, Facultad de Economía de la UNAM, (mimeo), 1985.

Ruiz, C.C. "Estructura productiva y distributiva de la región Centro de México," in *Diagnóstico del sistema de ciudades y descentralización en la región Centro de México.* CEDDU, El Colegio de México, (mimeo), 1985.

Sánchez, A.N. and Moreno, J.L. *La población de America Latina: bosquejo histórico.* Buenos Aires, Paidós, 1968.

Unikel, L., Ruiz, C. and Garza, G. *El desarrollo urbano de México*. México, El Colegio de México, 1976.
United Nations. *Modalidades del crecimiento de la población urbano y rural*. Nueva York S.79.X11.9. 1981.

3 Santo Domingo in Crisis

by
José Francisco Peña Gómez

Administering a city in a time of international economic crisis and swift population growth is the most difficult challenge a modern politician can undertake. As the President of Spain, Dr. Felipe González, said at a meeting with the Santo Domingo Municipal Council, "It is more difficult to administer a city than to govern a country."

Heads of state can govern away from the noise of the crowds, away from the critical poverty of the marginal population, away from the precarious slums and belts of misery around the megalopolises and metropolises of Third World countries. But a Latin American municipal administrator must have daily responses to the problems of marginality, whose violent tides shake the fragile ship of municipal administration. A mayor has to keep daily contact with the people and must have adequate responses to the problems and conflicts posed by poverty. Moreover, he has to solve them. Lack of adequate municipal resources does not justify lack of action.

I
Population Growth and Rapid Urbanization

Uncontrollable population growth is the fundamental factor which accounts for both the manageability of cities and the popular background of their mayors and aldermen. These have brought about a situation totally different from that of the past, during colonial times and the first decades of our republican life. This phenomenon has taken place in all continents and societies, but it is much more serious in Latin America, since our region has the most rapid urbanization.

As present Mayor of the City of Santo Domingo, and General Secretary of the principal political party of the last twenty years, a period during which our party has controlled the political life of Santo Domingo—which is our greatest electoral stronghold in the Dominican Republic—I have had the opportunity to witness the transformation of a small city into a metropolis, burdened by urban marginality, as a result of this unrestrained population growth. In 1950, the population of Santo Domingo City was only 181,550 inhabitants. In 1984, it is estimated that the metropolitan population is 1,600,000 inhabitants, while the total governed by the Government of the National District is 1,900,000 inhabitants. The projected population for the year 2000 is 4 million inhabitants.

The World Report 1984 of the World Bank states that accelerated demographic expansion started in the second half of the twentieth century. In the year 1 A.D., the world population was 300 million inhabitants. It took over 1,500 years to double that number. The population doubled again in a cycle of 750 years, ascending to 1.7 billion inhabitants in 1900, and the last duplication took place in only thirty years: from 1950 to the present, world population has increased from 2.5 billion to about 4.8 billion inhabitants.

Since the first half of this century, the greatest population growth has been centered in the developing countries, a fact which has worsened our economic and social problems. There is a marked difference between the processes of birth-rate growth in industrialized and Latin American countries. The demographic growth rate seldom reaches 1% in Europe and 1.5% in the United States, whereas in Latin America, the population/growth rate increased beyond 2% per year, reaching an average level of 2.4% in the 1960s. Probably the most important single reason for rapid population growth in the last decades is the extraordinary progress made in the field of medicine, which affected both developed and developing countries, and which destroyed the relative balance between birth-rate and death-rate that was the principal stabilizing population factor in the past.

I have always considered that the key to development lies in the education and social discipline of the people. Birth control by the peoples of industrialized countries has been self-imposed, to such an extent that certain countries such as France, after the World War, had to foster demographic growth by establishing grants in favor of those parents with many children. In the Third World, the inhabitants' unawareness of the negative effects of population growth upon economic development has been the efficient cause of the explosive population growth. Only those developing countries, such as the People's Republic of China, that have imposed a strict birth regulation by force, have achieved a population growth control compatible with the provision of investment resources.

It is difficult to govern a city at this juncture. It will be more so in the near future, since the World Bank predicts that world population will increase from 4.8 billion inhabitants to 11 billion inhabitants by the year 2150. Inequalities in wealth, education and life quality between the developed countries and the Third World nations will become unfathomable in the year 2050. While the population of the developed countries will increase about 200 million, going from 1.2 billion to 1.4 billion, the developing countries' population will spring from 3.6 billion to 8.4 billion inhabitants. If it is now difficult to provide transportation, food, clothing, education and work to the Third World population, it is easy to imagine the tremendous problems which governing the societies of the future will entail.

The greatest difficulties will confront the administrations of the cities in Latin America, the world region that has experienced the greatest degree of urbanization. In 1980, two-thirds of the Latin American population lived in cities, a level which the developed countries reached in 1950. Even countries of a high birth-rate, such as those in Asia and Africa, remain predominantly rural, since their urbanization level is only 25%.

The largest cities in the world are found in Latin America. In 1950 the population of the Mexico City Metropolitan Area was 3.1 million inhabitants. It is estimated that in 1984, the population is between 16 and 17 million inhabitants, and its projected population for the year 2000 is 30 to 31 million inhabitants.

This phenomenon of swift urbanization in Latin America deserves special study. The United Nations Economic Commission for Latin America (CEPAL) has recently published an interesting study on "The Dynamics and Structure of the Process of Human Settlement in Latin America and the Caribbean." CEPAL summarizes the problem in these terms: "The characteristics of the process of population settlement in the countries of the region are the rapid concentration rate of the population in one or two cities, the dispersion of rural population and establishment and growth of the so-called precarious human settlements." Another distinguishing trait of Latin American metropolitanization is "the acute centralization of control," a situation which is very different from that of Europe and the United States, where greater community autonomy and decentralization contributed to a more homogenous development.

There seems to be a correlation between demography and climate, because some inter-regional comparisons show that the greatest population growth in Latin America is centered in the tropical countries. Indeed, that rate for Central America and the Caribbean is far greater than the one belonging to the Southern Cone countries. Of course, this is due not only to climatic reasons, but also to the greater degree of education and socio-economic development in those nations.

Metropolitanization and rapid urbanization have been recent social phenomena. At the beginning of the century, Latin America did not have a single city with a population of one million inhabitants, whereas in 1980, there were 26 Latin American metropolises, defined, as the United Nations suggests, as urban settlements with more than a million inhabitants. The megalopolis, the name given to the largest urban concentrations, is "the most remarkable characteristic" of urbanization in Latin America.

The CEPAL study describes this phenomenon in the following terms:

In 1950, there were only two cities which had more than 10 million inhabitants, New York (12.3 million) and London (10.4). In 1980, there were ten such cities, among them, Mexico City (15.0), São Paulo (13.5), Rio de Janeiro (10.7), and Buenos Aires (10.1). In the forecasts for the year 2000, six cities of the region appear amongst the 35 greatest cities of the world. They are Mexico (31), São Paulo (25.8), Rio de Janeiro (19), Buenos Aires (12.1), Bogota (9.6) and Lima-Callao (8.6). It is estimated that in the period 1980-2000, the population of these six cities will increase from 59 to 109 millions, and the region will have the greatest human crowds in the world.

This explosive growth of the Latin American city is due to the fact that the capitals of our countries concentrate the highest degree of industrialization and, consequently, the power of offering jobs to the rural migrants.

A. Power Alberti, Director of the CEPAL Agency in Bogota, in a study entitled "the Metropolitanization Process in Latin America," pointed out that: "The socio-economic model prevailing in Latin America has been characterized by the accumulation of wealth and income, the regional concentration of productive activities and basic social services, and the overconcentration of political power and government expenditure; all these factors produced as a result a human settlement pattern which tends to concentrate as well."

II
Migration and Marginality

As Mayor of the City of Santo Domingo, I have had the opportunity to acquire a sound knowledge of the problems of the precarious human settlements that surround the city. These settlements are characterized by the presence of squatters who build dwellings, using pieces of wood, tin, asbestos, cement, or cardboard. They frequently improvise these dwellings overnight, to protect themselves from eviction by the authorities.

The Economic Commission for Latin America considers that more than 40% of the urban population in Latin America live in such precarious human settlements and in conditions of poverty. It is estimated that in the year 2000, the urban population imprisoned in the web of poverty will reach two thirds of the total.

Rural migration, one of the causes of the metropolitanization of the continent, is partly due to unequal economic development. While the cities have entered the field of capitalism, with its modern industrial installations, the rural Latin American areas show a backwardness which has lasted for centuries. Their agriculture has not yet gotten rid of the most distinguishing marks of pre-capitalism. The roots of rural migration lie not only in land tenure but also in the archaic character of land exploitation, which lacks a modern concept of agricultural production and disregards modern technology.

The widespread use of multinational capital in the Latin American rural areas does not always represent progress from a social point of view, because this capitalist penetration materializes in the plantation form, precisely to take advantage of the low cost of labor. The absence of an adequate technology—the producer of well-paid jobs in the country—compels the laborers to search for better opportunities beyond the occupational capacity of the "local baron."

Apart from the outdated techniques of land cultivation, rural migration may be also explained by the absence of electrical power, drinking water, schools, medical service and means of transportation which would make life easier for the rural dwellers. The fundamental difference in the urbanization process between Europe and the United States on the one hand and Latin America on the

other lies in the fact that the expansion of the cities in the industrialized countries was suitably accompanied by the extension of municipal services to the
periphery, where many of the community members dwell. By contrast, in the
Latin America metropolis, population growth has not been accompanied by the
necessary infrastructure to provide transportation, education, health care, road
and sewage systems and electrical power to the marginal population.

Latin America has witnessed the emergence of the "swollen city." This is a
completely different phenomenon even from the hypertrophic city of the past.
This latter developed continually, but always as a city meeting local conditions
and concepts concerning housing and public services. On the other hand, the
swollen city increased its population but did not provide the adequate infrastructure and neglected quality in housing.

These swollen cities are surrounded by indigent neighborhoods which are de-
void of fundamental services, such as drinking water, paved streets, sewage
systems, electrical power. This dreadful growth of some Latin American cities
is far from being a metropolitanization; it is rather a "gigantic marginality."
The overconcentration of the population has brought about very serious problems. Increasing delinquency prevails in the streets of big cities, where municipal or national police cannot cope with the crime which is fostered by unemployment and the hopeless living conditions of the marginal population.

The greatest challenge a municipality has to face is to bring into the framework of modern life this population, which has either been expelled from the
country and has settled in the periphery of our cities, or has been born within
the city itself as a gigantic crowd. As Mayor of the National District, where
the capital of the Dominican Republic lies, I have achieved a full understanding of the seriousness of the problem posed by urban marginality and of the im-
pending dangers which it entails for the stability of democratic order in Latin
America.

Much has been said recently about the need to level out unequal development,
and to focus attention on the rural areas, so as to stop the migratory wave that
invades the cities. This seems to be part of the policy of adjustment proposed by
the International Monetary Fund, which advises us to give back to the rural
dweller, in the form of fair prices and more efficient services, part of the lost
incentive to remain in this habitat. The problem is that they do so in a form
which will penalize the city dweller.

The marginal population of the city, as opposed to the poor of the countryside, has stepped into civilization. They benefit from the access to the greater
information which is at the disposal of the city inhabitants. The constant sight
of the offensive wealth of the rich and powerful people who live in fashionable neighborhoods, and the sight of magnificent industrial and commercial installations, make a sharp contrast with their precarious life conditions. This
constitutes a permanent source of quiet fury and social resentment.

The situation of unemployment and social negligence which the poor of the
cities endure, added to the effects of constant indoctrination by activists belong-

ing to the most radical political organizations, may in the future contribute to the transference of the center of armed struggle from the rural areas to the city, a fact which will transform cities into an inferno of violence.

This violence, a direct result of the marginality of an important part of our city, is revealing itself at the social level. Personal violence is one of the direct consequences of marginality, which pits people with no resources against better-off groups. This phenomenon cannot be analyzed only from a political point of view because its causes are deeper. It requires a social-economic policy approach geared to diminish urban marginality.

The Dominican Republic is a typical example of accelerated urbanization and of disorderly population growth. The first census of population took place in 1920, when the percentage of rural population was 83%. Since that date, as has been pointed out by a study carried out by the Technical Secretariat of the Presidency:

> The proportion of urban population has increased enormously, from 16.6% in 1920, increasing to 23.8% in 1950 and reaching 52% in 1981. In 1920, there were only seven cities with a population over 5,000 inhabitants, with a combined population of 87,488 people. In 1981, there were 60 cities of that size, reaching a total population of 2,806,000. 47% of this increment in urban population was centered in Santo Domingo.

The growth rate of the majority of the urban centers rose during that period, to percentages within the 5-6% range per year, whereas the rate for the total population reached 3% per year.

The city of Santo Domingo has become one of the biggest of Central America and the Caribbean. In 1920, the city had just 31,000 inhabitants, whereas the National District now has a population of about 2,000,000 inhabitants. The growth of the city of Santo Domingo fluctuates between 6% and 7.15% per year.

The Dominican migrants come principally from other urban centers, as has been pointed out by the above-mentioned study of the Technical Secretariat of the Presidency. The number of people coming from rural areas is much smaller. 56.4% of the migrants in Santo Domingo come from "El Cibao," a region in the northern part of the country. This rural migration has a twofold effect. On the one hand, it depopulates the Dominican countryside. On the other hand, it impoverishes the rural areas since those who migrate are the better educated and, as a result, those who have the greatest capacity to produce.

The Department of Urban Planning of the Santo Domingo Municipal Government prepared a study, on my request, to identify the principal problems in the National District. They are: the lack of capacity of the urban economy to provide enough jobs for the population centered in Santo Domingo; an uneven population distribution in the urban area which creates problems of overcrowding and of extremely low density; a great concentration of population in areas whose topography makes it very difficult to provide basic services; the deterioration of the environment by pollution; a bad distribution of the infrastucture for basic services; the continuous increment of new urbanized areas without planning and, as a result, with very few possibilities for being helped in their development; a state of anarchy in the distribution of urban land (residential, commercial, industrial, etc.); the uncontrollable and accelerated appearance of low-income settlements; the inadequate use of public roads; a crowding produced by the commercialization and distribution of the agricultural production of the whole country; and finally great speculation in urban land prices.

Another study, carried out by us recently, on the urban problems states that:

Santo Domingo has developed with no planning at all, thus the use of the land is the result of a nonplanned organization which responds to the characteristics of urban activity. The city grew having as a starting point the area which is still today the most important business center. The physical characteristics of the city have conditioned the possession of its territory. The plots of land that are located to the West and North-West of the center have been traditionally occupied by the upper class as a result of their topography and landscape, while the plots of land to the North and North-East are occupied by the lower income groups. The development of the city has been characterized by a low housing density. Single family housing, with a garden and a yard, is predominant. 39.7% of the population of Santo Domingo occupies 83.3% of its lands.

Since a house is occupied by one household, the city of Santo Domingo has an extension of almost 200 square kilometers. This low density makes it impossible to offer the inhabitants of the slums adequate sanitary services, health services, housing services and transportation services.

The resources of the Santo Domingo municipal government are insufficient to aid the lowest income households of the slums, and at the same time to offer efficient services to the residents of the urban center and the residential areas, who do not pay the real value of these services. As a result of this, the municipal government is facing a very serious economic situation, made even worse by the crisis that the Dominican Republic, like all Latin American countries, is suffering nowadays.

In 1963, the municipal budget amounted to RD $8.4 million, at a time when there was parity between the Dominican peso and the American dollar. The City of Santo Domingo had only 511,000 inhabitants then. Thus the average citizen received RD $16.4 in services. In 1982, with a budget of RD$18.3 million, the number of inhabitants had increased more than three times, reaching 1.6 million. As a consequence, the expenditure per inhabitant was reduced to RD $11.4. This situation is even more dramatic if we take into consideration the figures in real terms, discounting from nominal expenditure the increase in the cost of living using the general index of consumer prices. According to the best sources of available information the real expenditure per inhabitant was reduced from RD $16.4 in 1963 to RD$10.4 in 1971 and to approximately RD $3.4 in 1982. This means that, if 1963 prices had been maintained, the municipal budget per inhabitant would have been reduced to one-fifth of its original level. In other words, population growth together with rising prices eliminated the effect of the nominal increments in the budget. With the available resources in 1982, the municipal government was able to offer a fifth of its services. The situation becomes even worse when we take into account the fact that municipal workers' salaries were increased threefold during that period, thus diminishing drastically the resources for investment. Conditions are even worse in 1984, when we have a budget of approximately RD $25 million, but in a currency devalued three times in relation to the dollar, for an administration that has had to face an inflationary process never experienced before.

Having to face problems as great and urgent as those posed by as big a metropolis as Santo Domingo, a municipal authority must be ready to carry out emergency plans. These require the utilization of aid provided by the private sector, by communities themselves, by the Central Government and by international cooperation.

One of the first things I did after I took office as Mayor of our capital was to create an Entrepreneurial Council of Municipal Assistance, made up of distinguished businessmen. This council has cooperated efficiently with municipal programs in favor of the lowest-income residents, as well as in those tending to improve the working conditions of municipal workers, who were the most badly paid civil servants.

The Entrepeneurial Council, following a request of mine, put together the resources to provide thousands of workers with boots and uniforms, to buy lawn mowers to be used in the city green areas, to set up libraries in the slums, to raise money to buy trucks at preferential prices from the New York City government, and to gather enough cash for the preparation of small baskets to be given to poor women on Mother's Day. The Entrepeneurial Council has also cooperated with the municipal government to collect considerable amounts of money, which have allowed the distribution of free food to the lowest income families. Last year we were able to distribute 35,000 boxes of food among the poorest people and this year we intend to increase these donations.

To complement the resources of the municipal government, we have also created neighborhood dwellers' associations, called *Juntas de Vecinos* the leaders of which cooperate with the authorities in works that are beneficial for their communities. In the cases in which they do not do the work themselves, their suggestions help the Municipal Executive and the Municipal Council to establish, in a better way, the priorities for government action.

Lacking resources on the national level, notwithstanding the generosity and understanding of the President, my friend Jorge Blanco, we have had to ask for international help, taking advantage of the excellent relations we have with parties and governments of the Socialist International, principally with countries of Western Europe. In this way, we have obtained a fleet of trucks used for public services and garbage removal, several vans used for transporting the technical staff, and donations of food and medicines.

The governments that have excelled in giving help have been those of the President of France, Francois Mitterrand; the President of the Italian Council, Bettino Craxi; Prime Minister Olaf Palme of Sweden, and the President of Spain, Felipe González.

Even more important than the foreign and national donations, and the subsidies from the Government, has been the fact that I have been able to keep control of the City of Santo Domingo, thus creating a reputation of good administration, thanks to the firmness with which I have confronted urban problems and to a complete dedication to my work. We have made up for the lack of adequate equipment by optimizing the equipment we have, and for this reason we ordered two work-shifts with different personnel. We have behaved with firmness to eliminate all abuses, whether they be committed by the rich or the poor. With equal determination we have demolished the fences of luxurious mansions that had converted ample zones of the beach nearest to Santo Domingo City into an exclusive center, and have also demolished thousands of shacks and rickety kiosks that stretched all over the commercial streets of Santo Domingo giving them a terribly shabby look. We eliminated all kiosks from the avenues of the capital and we relocated the vendors in hygienic stalls that have made the city extremely attractive and picturesque.

Since we understand that one of the most fundamental problems of marginality and poverty is the lack of technical ability for productive work, we set up the so-called "Labor Schools." In them, women acquire the basic knowledge of handicrafts and handiwork, thus becoming productive beings in society. In coordination with distinguished members of the private sector, we contributed to the creation of an Association of Micro-Enterprises, which, due to its excellent success in the capital, has spread all over the country and is receiving the attention of international institutions that regard this association as a model against urban marginality. We have also set up popular libraries for those children who do not have texts and we have fought delinquency by building dozens of sports clubs.

These solutions are very restrictive since perhaps they do not attack the roots of the problems but their effects. We believe that to abolish marginality in the short term it is necessary to control population growth, to execute the reforms that the Latin American peasants wait for and need, to promote agricultural development and also industrial development, particularly in the medium sized cities, which act as transfer stations for the migrants from the countryside. A national mobilization and the utilization of the community's own resources, including communal work, would place local governments in a position in which they would be able to confront the problem of urban marginality.

The governments of the industrialized nations should cooperate in helping us to solve this problem. The problem, indeed, is not only ours, but also is a problem for rich countries, since the great capitals of the industrialized powers are the last stopping-off point in the complete journey of international migration. The absence of a solution to the problems of marginality and of poverty in the neighboring countries to the United States has been the cause of the great exodus of our nationals toward American territory.

In the Dominican Republic there exists an organized clandestine traffic of illegal immigrants to Puerto Rico, the compulsory stopping point on the road to New York City. Exactly the same happens along the extensive border between Mexico and the United States.

Any investment which the United States may make by means of direct economic assistance, to help us solve the problems posed by marginality, will help to stop the surge of economic exiles who arrive daily at its shores and airports and who impair, with their presence, the conditions of life in North American society, bringing to the surface or deepening existing social differences. The United States does not have boundless resources, and unless it agrees upon concerted action with neighboring countries to face seriously the phenomena of metropolitanization and marginality, it will not be able to avoid the transfer of this problem to its territory, with all the negative consequences this entails.

To put an end to marginality, it is necessary to reestablish justice in international trade, so that the Latin American countries may obtain fairer prices for their raw materials, not only from the United States but also from the European Economic Community. It is also necessary that the United States and the Soviet Union put an end to the arms race, which consumes hundreds of billions of dollars, so that a part of those resources which are wasted in the manufacture of weapons to destroy human civilization may be devoted to make life easier and safer for the poor of the world. The transfer of technology is another factor which may help us control the inordinate growth of our cities, since greater experience and more advanced scientific development may guide us better in the field of urban growth.

Population growth was controlled in the first seventeen centuries of the Christian era by the balancing devastation of epidemics, wars, and infant mortality. Progress in medicine made epidemics disappear, although a new world war could wipe out the human race from the face of the planet. To control population we can only resort to the very scientific means which served to accelerate its growth. We should be able to bury all deadly weapons in the depths of the earth and of the sea. We should be able to transform them into tractors, schools, hospitals, new industries and research projects, to develop new technologies for the production of food and the building of low cost housing.

We are destined to fulfill this task, because doing the opposite would transform the leaders of today's nations into perpetrators of genocide. Nuclear annihilation will not leave survivors on earth.

We must not become suicides, making the marvelous structure of human civilization collapse upon ourselves.

4 The New York Fiscal Crisis and its Lessons for Latin American Cities

by Matthew Edel

I
Introduction

Surpassed by Mexico City and Sao Paulo, New York is no longer the Western Hemisphere's largest city. Nonetheless, it remains the world's financial center; the magnet for immigration; the United Nations headquarters and a major center of culture and communication. With over seven million inhabitants, it is still one of the great "World Cities" (Hall, 1966).

New York is also an enduring source of the symbols and lessons which set the tone for other cities. London and New York were the first cities to cope with four million people. Greater London and Greater New York pioneered metropolitan consolidation and large integrated subway systems. New York shares with Chicago the claim for the introduction and spread of the skyscraper. The names of neighborhoods, from "Wall Street" to "Coney Island," from "Harlem" to "Scarsdale," symbolize their functions for the world.

New York is also a warning, both symbolic and practical. The introduction of skyscrapers elsewhere leads to debates over "Manhattanization." Preachers and politicians point to New York as a negative example of alienation and avarice, crime and lust. To this list of warnings, another was added in the 1970s: New York as the scene of excessive public spending and borrowing, of an over-ambitious public agenda, and a subsequent brush with bankruptcy. Not to be like New York became the watchword for fiscal prudence throughout the land, the warning impelling caps on spending.

This article will examine the New York fiscal crisis as symbol and concrete lesson, in the light of a more recent episode: the Latin American debt crisis. The near default and subsequent restructuring of Mexico, Brazil and their neighbors came seven years after the New York bailout. The parallel between the two events is close, despite the obvious differences between the most central of cities and the nations of the periphery. Latin America's problems reinforce the interpretation that New York City's troubles were not just a result of purely idiosyncratic government behavior. They also feed into a new debate as to whether New York is becoming more like a Third World metropolis. For the nations and cities of Latin America, New York stands as an example of the kinds of interpretation and misinterpretation of cause and blame which can be expected to influence policy. Beyond that, the specific means of coping that unfolded in New York can yield useful lessons.

The next section of this paper considers the overall economic background of New York. I then turn to the interpretations of New York's difficulties that were offered at the time of the fiscal crisis, and argue that subsequent history argues for an interpretation that stresses outside forces in the economic cycle, rather than placing all of the blame on internal political actors. Then I look at specific actions taken by New York in resolving or coping with the crisis, looking specifically for those lessons and warnings that might be useful for Latin America. Finally, I discuss the debate on whether the parallel financial crises reinforce an argument that New York is becoming more like the Third World cities.

II
The New York Background

New York was one of several maritime centers that grew on the Atlantic coast of British North America prior to independence. With the coming of the Republic, New York used a combination of political connections, strategic public works investments, the natural advantages of its port, and its potential access to the Midwest to secure a position as the nation's largest city and economic center (Albion, 1984; Kouwenhoven, 1953).

The Two New Yorks
New York grew rapidly from the 1820s to the 1920s. First the city proper on the island of Manhattan, next the city of Brooklyn across the East River and then the surrounding counties of New York State gained population. In 1898, New York, Brooklyn and three other counties were merged under one municipal government. The century of growth brought the city's population to eight million people. Including the nearby New Jersey cities, and the outer suburbs to the North and on Long Island as well as in Connecticut and New Jersey, the metropolitan area had over fifteen million people by 1956 (See Table 1). Some commentators even spoke of an entire urbanized northeast Megalopolis, a corridor following the railroad connecting Washington, Philadelphia, New York and Boston (Hoover and Vernon, 1959; Editors of Fortune, 1958).

This growth was initially linked to port activities. As the city grew, two principal activities emerged from the shipping-related nexus. On the one hand, to shipping and stevedoring were added industrial activities, catering in part to trade and in part to a local or regional market. This blue collar New York was swelled by immigrants. Wave upon wave arrived from Europe's loci of economic and political disruption: from Ireland and Germany in the mid-19th century; from Eastern Europe and Italy at the century's close. Smaller but substantial streams came from virtually everywhere else. By 1950, the city held about a million industrial jobs, and a couple of hundred thousand blue collar jobs in transportation. New York became particularly important as a center for the

Table 1

Population by Borough/County (1000s)

	1956	1970	1980	1990 est
N.Y. City	7791	7952	7116	7165
Manhattan	1811	1539	1428	1430
Bronx	1427	1472	1169	1158
Brooklyn	2616	2602	2231	2260
Queens	1729	1987	1891	1920
Staten Island	208	352	397	397
Suburbs	2383	3680	3733	3856
Nassau	1105	1429	1322	1320
Suffolk	443	1127	1284	1369
Westchester	724	894	867	880
Rockland	111	230	260	287

Sources: 1956: Hoover and Vernon (1959); 1970, 1980: US Census; 1990 estimate: Port Authority of New York and New Jersey.

garment industries, toys, jewelry, printing and smallscale metal-casting. Its industrial structure was marked by large numbers of small plants and firms rather than the few giants that dominated the steel and auto centers of the midwest (Hoover and Vernon, 1959).

The second New York was the city of finance. Growing out of the financing and insuring of the shipping trade, the financial center came to replace London as the money and stock market of the world economy. White collar jobs, from clerks and bookkeepers to lawyers and brokers, expanded and expanded. By the turn of the 20th century, financial leaders had supplanted shippers and manufacturers as the city's "business" leaders. Finance, rather than manufacturing, also came to be the major influence on those urban "service" sectors that grow to supply any growing local economic base: retail and entertainment, education and social services, real estate and public utilities and the like.

The two New Yorks coexisted uneasily. If Brazil has been described as "Belindia" (Belgian level industry surrounded by Indian level rural poverty), New York must be Switz-kong (Switzerland and Hong Kong). The two sectors competed for land, through market and political process. The first zoning codes were designed to keep garment manufacturing away from New York's fancy shop and financial districts. As early as the 1920s, organizations of the financial elite and their real estate allies began espousing plans to push the industrial and immigrant New York out of Manhattan. They also struggled over the shape and function of social service and social control institutions, from the City College system to the police force.

Nonetheless all was not open conflict. A number of political institutions, in and out of government, developed to mediate between the two New Yorks, and between the city's different economic strata.

The Mediating Institutions

The Democratic Party has dominated the city. At its most powerful, the Party was an amalgamation of ethnic-based political clubs, labor unions and utility and real estate contributors. Political leaders provided government and public utility jobs, as well as cash patronage for the first; a degree of municipal protection for the second; and specific favors for the third. At times, the party formed a single "machine"; with the later decomposition of the machine into rival cliques, the basic alliances nonetheless held, with the ostensibly separate groups forming what critics call a "permanent government" (Newfield and DuBruhl, 1978).

Financial and manufacturing leaders did not play as much of a role in local government as the other groups. As long as the city did not harass them too much, they did not challenge Democratic hegemony. They directed their main influence to national or state political campaigns, while pushing specific local policies through a variety of local voluntary organizations (The City Club, the Regional Plan Association for New York and its environs, and the like). In specific economic crises and periods of weak social control, however, they organized interludes of coalition ("fusion") leadership by business-led reform blocs.

The Postwar Cycle

The economic and demographic base of this system began to change after the Second World War. The opening of the surrounding counties linked to the city by highways, and the offering of homeownership underwritten by federal credit policies, led to massive suburbanization of population. In the inner areas of the city, new migrant streams from Puerto Rico and the "Black Belt" of the South supplanted earlier streams from Europe. After 1964, further currents from Latin America and Asia developed. The city's population fell from 8 million to 7 million, with a rising share from minority groups, even as the metropolitan area population continued to rise slowly. The number of jobs in the city fell only slightly, but the number of manufacturing jobs was rapidly reduced, from about a million to a quarter of that number today. More of the remaining jobs, mostly in offices, came to be held by suburban commuters. With the loss of industrial jobs, possibilities for advancement for new migrants were restricted, adding to poverty in the minority population.

These changes led to new demands on the public sector: for welfare and police expenditures to cope with poverty and its effects; for education to try to prepare some part of the population for new office jobs; and for new public facilities to cope with commuting demands (highways, mass transit, etc.), and with the office industry's demands for space (urban redevelopment programs). Politically, the disruption of older immigrant communities and manufacturing unions, and the increasingly international orientation of business, removed certain key actors from the old political coalition. Both old-line and reform politicians came to rely even more than before on real estate interests for funds. Of the political system's "popular" bases, only municipal employee unions and a few "old immigrant" communities whose residents had moved up to semi-professional positions were able to retain any influence on politics.

In an effort to satisfy or pacify its demographic constituencies, and to provide an attractive environment for business, commuters and real estate, the city government increased its expenditures in the 1950s and particularly the 1960s. For a time, the national economic boom contributed to adequate local revenues, while increased federal aid also allowed expansion. Additional funds, primarily for infrastructure, but to some extent for current expenses, were raised by borrowing. With the 1970s' slowdown of the economy, the conservative turn of federal aid under Richard Nixon's administration, and particularly the oil shock of 1973, the city could no longer maintain its expenses. Additional borrowing was attempted. But finally lenders refused to roll over old loans without a sharp change in terms. The city was declared to be in a "fiscal crisis:" in imminent danger of default.

A series of rescue packages, developed to prevent full and open bankruptcy, were implemented. New loans were made, with prior claims to city resources for their repayment. Boards and auditors representing creditors and the state and federal governments were to supervise "reforms," to reduce city expenditures and employment. Like the policy packages that Latin American and other debtor nations have to accept as a condition for IMF and bank loans, New York's "rescue" imposed as much general austerity as could be induced at the municipal level. The significant exception was that, not being a sovereign state with a central bank, New York could not be required to reduce its money supply. (Alcaly and Mermelstein 1976; Feretti 1976; Newfield and DuBruhl, 1978; Auletta, 1980; Tabb 1982; Bailey, 1984; Lichten, 1986.)

III
The Debate over Causality

New York's fiscal crisis gave rise to a heated debate about why "it" had happened "here." Critics and defenders of the city—and there were both of these both on the right and on the left—offered a number of arguments about causes of the crisis.

The Conservative Critique
In one set of arguments, the city's government, politicians and unions were blamed for demanding too much for social services. The argument is encapsulated in such book titles as "The Cost of Good Intentions" and "The Streets Were Paved with Gold" (Morris 1980; Auletta, 1980; see also Starr, 1985). *Fortune Magazine* argued at the time, "New York is a special case. New York is different because it has had a credit card that enabled it to live beyond its means" (Robertson, 1975). The city government's own Temporary Commission on City Finances (1978) claimed that the problem was the result of recent local extravagance which could be corrected by fiscal austerity. Up to 1965, they said, New

York had 20 years of "relatively stable" politics and finances. Only some of the city's problems—referred to as historical burdens—had emerged earlier.

The commission cited several "recent" problems: high taxes, high expenditure levels, a high debt burden. The use of borrowed funds for current expenses and increases in pension benefits were particularly criticized as involving a burden on future budgets. Waste and excessive generosity to labor and to service recipients were cited as the factors underlying all of these problems. A typical example is the commission's argument that "because pension improvements, unlike salary increases, do not have to be funded immediately, city officials were able to defer payments into the future while reaping short-term political benefits such as municipal union support in electoral politics" (Temporary Commission, 1978). This view was also reflected in speeches by then-President Gerald Ford and other officials.

Two Radical Critiques

This conservative orthodoxy was sometimes countered by a radical alternative. This also stressed short term malfeasance, but attributed it to the political machine, along with bankers and real estate interests, who spent too much on graft and on tax-exemptions, giveaways and luxury public works for the rich and powerful (Newfield and DuBruhl, 1978; Fitch, 1976).

A different political-economic critique was that the crisis was the result of external events in the national or world economy. These had shown their effects first in New York, for partially idiosyncratic reasons, but they were affecting all cities to some extent. This view saw the New York crisis in terms of the city's role in the post-World-War II "long boom" of the American economy, and in the downturn in that boom that was already apparent at the time of the city crisis. This "radical" analysis, which drew on Shumpeterian and neo-Marxian thought, focused on the institutional arrangements of the postwar boom, and on the way in which the boom and those arrangements affected both the general crisis and the city's role in it (Edel 1976; Gordon 1977 and 1978; Tabb 1982; Bowles, Gordon and Weiskopf, 1983; Lichten, 1986).

The Long Cycle View of The Boom

In the long cycle view, the postwar boom had several key features. The first was the linking together of the Western powers and the dependent Third-World economies into one economic system, under the leadership of United States capital. This world order was marked by the expansion of large corporations and financial institutions, by the establishment of a new division of labor at the international level, by increased international movement of raw materials and many finished goods, and by economies of large-scale production of some goods in the developed areas. It also expanded the production of other goods by low-paid labor in peripheral areas and by relatively low-paid migrants in industrial centers, and destroyed economic opportunities for much of small business.

A second aspect was the creation of labor-market and social-welfare institutions to guarantee a steady supply of labor and general public order in the capitalist centers. The recognition of labor unions in the United States, their growth elsewhere, and the spread of the welfare state, were all results of the Depression and World War II. Some specific institutions primarily served to mitigate class conflict, to seek "legitimation" of the system, in James O'Connor's terminology (1973).

Schools, welfare programs and other government services also sought to channel labor to the needs of industry. The same was true of such institutions as seniority contracts, industrial pensions and federal home-mortgage subsidies, which gave workers specific incentives to maintain continuous employment. The programs thus also served O'Connor's "accumulation" function: direct assistance to capitalist growth. Macroeconomic policy and planning efforts also served to prevent economic disorder and to reduce competition among capitalists. In recent political economy these institutions are described as fostering an "autocentric" growth cycle with high wages stimulating demand and technological change and hence growth in the "center" nations. They are thus sometimes presented as a permanent "structural" feature of capitalism at the center (Amin 1976; de Janvry 1981). A more convincing interpretation sees them as a result of class struggles and compromises in a historically specific environment (Przeworski, 1985; Edel, Sclar and Luria 1985).

Part of this environment, a third aspect of the postwar boom, was the growth of the petroleum-based and technological complex. Petroleum-using means of road, air and sea transportation expanded the international division of labor and allowed the reorganization of urban housing over larger areas. Tractors, fertilizers and insecticides allowed mechanization of agriculture and the introduction of fertilizer-dependent hybrid grains. These major innovations, along with new materials and electronics, provided the technical basis for cheaper production of machinery and consumer necessities. Thus, for at least some workers in the developed capitalist countries, living standards could be increased, while at the same time profit rates could recover from the depression and maintain themselves at a high level. The new technologies, including military hardware, also allowed efficient repression of those areas of the world not benefiting by the rising living standards, and of occasional dissidents in the industrial centers.

Related to these three aspects was the ability of the United States to maintain labor discipline by means of opportunities for individual mobility. People worked hard attempting to better their personal or family positions. Education, movement from blue- to white-collar jobs, and migration from farm to city or from city to suburb, were all possible for enough individuals to keep others striving. As long as general productivity grew, administrative work expanded and new technology created jobs for those trained, mobility could remain credible. The system of social control by mobility was less successful outside of the United States, and an attempt to export it to the weaker capitalist nations in the Alliance for Progress failed completely. Even in the United States some groups were excluded, and there was always some tendency for new occupations, suburbs and educational credentials to decline in value as more people came to possess them (Edel, Sclar and Luria, 1984).

By the 1970s, the main causes of the boom had begun to erode. First, United States dominance over a capitalist world economy had been weakened. The rebellions of the dependent nations, most dramatic in the victory of the Indochinese revolutions, raised the cost of maintaining empire. Even the most conservative of national leaders were emboldened to raise prices of natural resources or use tariffs to promote industrial modernization. Among developed nations, the United States lost power relative to Europe and Japan. Rising costs and increasing competition, emerging when corporations become multinational enough to move capital easily across borders, limited the extent to which surplus could be devoted by corporations or governments to the creation of new jobs and opportunities in the capitalist centers.

Second, the technological supports of the boom had passed the point at which increasing productivity can allow simultaneous increases in both living standards and profits. Further, the labor-channeling institutions that worked well in the first two postwar decades themselves revealed their contradictions. Use of school and welfare systems to contain large numbers of people temporarily or permanently out of production provoked the response of mass student and welfare-rights movements. Labor unions, content with productivity bargaining when productivity was outstripping the cost of living, demanded gains that kept up with inflation when productivity fell behind. The promise of mobility for all could not be kept, by its very nature; even small tokens of mobility became more costly as other aspects of the boom faced their difficulties. Individual and group alienation and dissatisfaction began to interfere with production and to require new and costly institutions for control, such as drug programs.

Whether one poses the problem in Schumpeterian terms as the end of the electronics/petroleum growth cycle, or in Marxian terms, as an exhaustion of the counteracting forces to falling profit rates, the result is clear. Growth became more difficult for the United States starting in the mid-1960s, and for Western Europe and Japan in the 1970s.

Problems of the Downswing

This posed, for the capitalist system, a problem which had emerged periodically before in history: how to stave off or cope with an economic slowdown that imposed either declining profits or reduced wages, that increased possibilities of social and international conflict and that threatened financial crisis. There were, to be sure, some differences between this and earlier crises. The economic and political configuration of the period was marked by powerful monopolies in many areas of production, by strong and economically active states mindful of the dangers of international retaliation, and by stronger unions than had existed in earlier economic crises. Perhaps as a result, inflationary finance and competitive devaluations were used, instead of wage reductions and tariff wars, to protect capital from threatened insolvency. These offsets did not solve the crisis of profitability. But they did stave it off, at the "cost" of a major explosion of world liquidity.

A number of authors, with David Harvey (1982) perhaps the most lucid, have pointed to credit expansion as a natural result of conditions of falling profitability. This "overaccumulation" means the mass of profits still is high, or is artificially inflated by monetary expansion, in a situation in which familiar industrial investment opportunities have dried up. In this situation, credit may find its way into real estate, commodity or stock booms, or into massive rushes of credit for what appear to be promising borrowers. (Thus, since the late 1960s, money in the United States has gone into agricultural land booms, urban real estate booms, commodity and stock market booms, municipal and foreign debt booms, and highly leveraged corporate mergers and buyouts.) Each boom tends to overextend itself and leave bankruptcies in its wake. As each sector collapses, the entire economic system is threatened with financial ruin, but may be saved by managed bailouts and a new extension of credit. What is more, any particular collapse or rescue can be used to beat down costs, by lowering expectations or wages or by enforcing technical or institutional restructuring (Lichten, 1986). This does not mean the entire process is stage-managed for that reason, but the net effect can help restore part of the system's profitability.

New York's Role in the Cycle

New York's period of extended borrowing, and its subsequent insolvency, can be seen as one of these credit booms and busts. The parallels between New York's cycle and the Latin American debt cycle reinforce this impression. But the question still remains why New York was the scene of one of the first major cycles of the type, in this particular period of recession and credit inflation.

Here we may turn to the role of cities, and particularly major financial centers, in the postwar boom. Both the institutional and the technological arrangements of the boom created a new spatial division of labor with contradictory roles for cities.

Among technological innovations, the automobile increased surburban housing opportunities for workers, but did so in a way that removed the housing of higher-wage workers, professionals and managers from the urban tax base, and weakened the cohesion of older neighborhoods. Further, subsidy policy favored radial highways and suburban mortgages over the public transit and quality public housing which could have ensured the urban centers' attractiveness.

Agricultural innovation also impelled cities into crisis. Improvements in agricultural productivity and the use of mechanical equipment and chemicals, assisted by migrant labor at peak seasons, drove large numbers of workers from agriculture. Mechanization and migration were intensified by federal policy for subsidies, government investment and technical assistance that favored larger farms, and by a deliberate mechanization that Southern farmers adopted in response to militancy by Black labor beginning in the 1950s. Many of the migrants found their way to cities in the North.

New York had coped successfully with large migrations of unskilled labor before. But by the 1960s, manufacturing jobs and chances for mobility into small business ownership had decreased. With older forms of employment and advancement limited, it fell to government to cope with the migrants, by training them for skilled occupations, by providing direct relief, or by repression of discontent. These tasks, being less important at earlier times, had been left to local governments when major economic policies were transferred to higher levels of government. This left them tied to a local tax base which was, however, already weakened by suburbanization and the decline of urban industry. Initially this created a fiscal crisis only in the narrow sense of a need to find national or regional taxing systems to tap a growing economy for local funds. With the end of the boom, the problem grew more serious.

The fiscal problems of New York seemed manageable, at first, because of the city's unique place in the postwar capitalist system. America's rise to world dominance had also meant the rise of New York as financial center for the world. Employment in financial, insurance and real-estate firms rose from 336,200 in 1950 to 459,600 in 1970; employment in headquarters of industrial firms from 76,900 in 1962 to 83,900 in 1968. Taxation of these activities was sometimes difficult, as Mayor Lindsay discovered when he first proposed a stock-transfer tax, but at least they brought some payroll and sales-tax revenues to the city, and kept real-estate values and taxes high.

The economic base was, however, inherently unstable. The activities expanding in New York were financed out of profits made elsewhere. As a result New York was sensitive to business cycles, but in a way that was not initially apparent.

Headquarters and auxiliary employment in New York, as well as high-rise construction employment, expanded throughout the boom. Even in the early stages of recession, New York's financial activities retained their profitability. In the early 1970s, inflation was fueled both by world capitalist financial arrangements to avoid a liquidity crisis and by domestic financing of the Vietnam war, domestic social programs and corporate bailouts. Increases in paper wealth, coming at a time in which profitable investment outlets were limited, created pools of mobile financial capital seeking some sort of outlet. Many of these funds found their way into the creation of new conglomerate and multinational enterprises. These served, at first, a function of centralization of capital: the wiping out and milking of smaller or obsolete enterprises, and the centralization of production into new and perhaps eventually more efficient centers. In the past this had generally been left to bankruptcy during crises. This new centralization brought to New York even more control over world business than it had previously had. As the Fortune 500 largest corporations increased the share of business they controlled, New York increased its share of the 500 with head offices in the city.

This consolidation also attracted to New York and other business centers a large amount of capital seeking profitable outlets for investment in real estate. In the late 1960s, office buildings found a ready market among corporate clients and independent businesses that served the major headquarters. Tax loopholes, deliberately designed to increase profits and investment, also helped make high-rise construction a desirable "shelter." As a result, big city skylines were transformed, and real-estate values generally inflated, leading to speculative stockpiling of older buildings. The increase in downtown values—apparently a renaissance of the older central cities—made the cities themselves appear to be good credit risks. Capital in search of profitable investment began to seek out tax-free municipal and state bonds as part of the urban construction boom. Public-sector expansion thus could join with private construction to create an apparent boom in the major cities, including New York, while the economy as a whole slipped into crisis.

The expansion of credit delayed the onset of crisis in New York. But when the 1973 oil price shock was added to other recessionary forces, corporate headquarters also faced crisis and had to cut back. The result was a sudden decline of office employment and a stagnation of tax revenues, just when costs rose most rapidly and loans became hard to get. As a result, crisis came suddenly rather than as a slow erosion of revenues and the job base. This, in turn, allowed the imposition of lower living standards on New Yorkers to be depicted ideologically as a necessary result of local government overexpansion rather than as an incident in general capitalist stagnation (Tabb 1982; Lichten, 1986).

This argument made it easier to argue for tight restrictions on the city, to be enforced by outside boards, because the city might not be trusted to reform itself. Thus the city first had to empower a new body, the Municipal Assistance Corporation (M.A.C.) representing creditor banks and national corporations, to sell its refinancing bonds. Later, when state aid was required, an Emergency Financial Control Board was created with some overlap in members with the earlier M.A.C. board, and later federal aid was conditioned on further supervision of the city. As a result, the city government's options for how to cut costs or raise further revenue were severely limited.

The Conservative Reply

The interpretation presented here suggests that the argument that austerity is the necessary result of local malfeasance is a case of "blaming the victim." (Tabb, 1976). The Temporary Commission, typical of conservative analysts, was contemptuous of views like this, calling them a "captive of events" theory—one that denies the influence of local government actions. This is not to say they argued against the importance of outside influences. These factors, they admitted

...could be construed to support a "captive of events" theory of the fiscal crisis in which the City of New York is conceived of as having little or no

*control over the events leading to the fiscal crisis. The "captive of events"
theory is a popular one that is true in some respects. The City of New York
largely was unable to control the transformations that occurred in the local
population and economy or the inter-governmental relations process. (Temporary Commission 1978).*

However, the Commission then rejected the theory because of its consequences. They called it an alibi, which "tends to absolve local political leaders of
responsibility for the fiscal crisis and buttresses the also-popular view that
the solution...lies in increased federal and state aid." In a masterpiece of in-
nuendo, they added, "The 'captive of events' theory thus has political as well
as theoretical underpinnings." The theory was pronounced guilty by association
and dismissed. (DeKadt et al. 1981).

The parallels between New York and the recent Latin American situation are
good arguments against this dismissal. Countries with very different histories
and forms of government are all in the same predicament that affected cities
and corporations in the developed nations. Logically, the prevalence of these
crises and controls should indicate that more than local malfeasance is at issue.
However, the IMF and other lenders treat with each country one by one, pre-
suming that each, separately, has invited trouble by overextending government
expenditures and the money supply, supporting high wages, and over-
regulating and overprotecting the economy. The first lesson from New York's experience is thus a warning to Latin America against such blaming of the victim.

IV
The New York Response

In the decade since the fiscal crisis, New York has become a symbol again:
the repentant sinner that has seen the error of its ways. The city has reduced its
expenditures, resumed payment of its restructured debt, retired some bonds
ahead of schedule and even gone back cautiously into the bond market. Since
1980, the city has undergone a new round of economic growth, albeit one limited
to sectors serving the city's "world center" role and associated luxury consumption (Sassen-Koob, 1984). The message purveyed is that by "taking its medicine" and reducing city expenditures, putting some caps on wages and pension
contributions, New York has restarted growth. The alternative possibility,
that the regrowth of the world-city economy stems largely from outside forces,
including the continued inflation of the world financial system, is not explored.
Nor is much said about the failure of the recovery to reach a large portion of
the city's population, as witnessed by the growing number of homeless individuals and families.

If the oversimplified lesson that "taking one's medicine will bring prosperi-
ty" is resisted, the New York response to crisis does bear useful lessons for other

cities and nations which are forced to undergo austerity programs. New York City has had to cope with some of the same issues that have since become familiar in Latin America: negotiation with creditors or their surrogates; internal struggle or compromise over the distribution of burdens, and the management of program and service retrenchment. Although the specific institutions of a United States city are different in many ways from those of Latin American nations or cities, the New York experience does suggest some lessons, or at least point to certain pitfalls and raise certain questions for Latin America.

Negotiating the Crisis

Whatever the underlying causes of insolvency, the specific outbreak of crisis in New York and in Latin America was a voluntaristic move by creditors. Any debtor whose revenues fall behind debt service, is, of course, potentially in trouble. But as long as creditors are willing to extend new loans and roll over old ones, immediate problems can be deferred. Reasons for new credit may be economic or political. Lenders still hope the debtor will secure new sources of revenue; the debtor may not be allowed to fail because this will stir up political waters or the debtor may be kept afloat specifically to defer the perception of crisis. The perceptions, political or economic, that lead to these credits being extended may of course be realistic or exaggerated.

The eventual cessation of credit may also be economic or political. Creditors may find their own resources strained; they may not be able to sustain a reasonable faith in the debtor's recovery; or they may decide to end credit to teach the debtor or other observers a political lesson.

In the New York case, Eric Lichten has argued, the timing of the crisis was specifically controlled by a group of leading investment and commercial banks. These first refused rollover credits to an autonomous construction agency of the New York State government, the Urban Development Corporation, and raised interest rates to the city. Then they refused rollover loans entirely, until the city accepted new forms of supervised austerity. Lichten argues that the timing was designed to make New York an example, a tryout case for the imposition of "austerity regimes" in other cities and states and then nationally (in the later Reagan cutbacks), with the aim of restoring corporate and bank profitability at a national level (Lichten, 1986).

Bankers, of course, hold that their timing was imposed by myriad small depositors throughout the country, who individually and simultaneously became fearful of New York notes because of the size of the city's deficit (Starr, 1985; Feretti, 1976). This position ignores the role of banks and bank-related rating services in providing the information that fed depositor fears. Another possibility is that bank rules-of-thumb, rather than specific planning, may have been involved at first.

Once triggered, however, the crisis quickly took on political coloration, whatever political calculation had been involved at first. After the initial increase in interest rates, banks had to choose either to continue to roll over loans and fund the city deficit, even at higher interest rates, or to refuse entirely to do so. They formed a Financial Community Liaison Group as an informal coordinating body. Once the initial refusal of credits had been made, the city and then the state were induced to set up formal bodies, the Municipal Assistance Corporation and the Emergency Financial Control Board, with participation by bankers and other business leaders, to oversee the city's behavior as a condition for new loans and loan extensions.

In the negotiation that followed, the banks were able to maintain a united stance, except on one occasion when a specific savings bank refused a compromise involving automatic rollover for a year of some bonds it held. (This opposition was not enough to disrupt the general trend of negotiation.) The banks' power was dominant since they had the money, the unity of action and the initial control over timing, as well as because of the general business oriented culture of the United States. The creditors were thus able to dominate the media's presentation of events to the public and largely to manipulate the terms under which the resolution occurred. Supervision of the city by the new boards, the imposition of severe cutbacks and the strengthening nationally of an aura that austerity was necessary all resulted.

On the other hand, the city was able to preserve its basic governmental and collective bargaining institutions under the new regime. The City Comptroller and many of the trade union leaders then in office are still in their posts a decade later, although the Mayor at the time was not reelected. Unions of city employees were able, at least partially, to minimize wage reductions (and keep their bargaining status), albeit at the cost of loss of many members' jobs. City officials were able to control many of the detailed allocations of retrenchment. Nor did the internal allocation of power between different ethnic constituencies change greatly. The white middle class exodus to the suburbs was accelerated, but not so greatly that upper class "gentrification" or "return to the city" would be discouraged when financial center employment began to expand again in the 1980s. This fundamental maintenance of control in the face of austerity may be deplored or applauded. The mayor who took over partway through the crisis has provided his own cheering section (Koch 1984). Lichten faults the unions for their complicity and his pessimism is borne out by increasing homelessness and rising income disparity in the post-crisis period of ostensible recovery.

How New York was able to develop its own negotiating coalition is primarily a story of the unions' role in the crisis. Union leaders became key players in the negotiations, coupling threats of strikes (but few actual strikes) with a promise to limit rank and file militancy if they were given a place at the expanded bargaining table brought about by the crisis. Pension funds, whose participation they could have vetoed, became key buyers of the new debt instruments created. From the unions' viewpoint, their action avoided a situation which could have been much worse.

This history can have only general lessons for other debtors, because historical specifics vary. But the general lessons are important. Debtor-creditor bargaining is not foreordained by any simple economic formula: it takes place in a political setting. In Latin America, as in New York, creditors had, to some extent, the choice of timing, and they were able to combine established institutions (the I.M.F.) with new consortia of banks. The debtors, on the other hand, have not been able to take advantage of whatever negotiating power a more unified consortium approach would give them. Internally, they have also varied in the extent to which they have been able to propose alternatives to the standard deflationary medicine proffered by the I.M.F. The New York experience suggests that internal cohesion and other political factors may be important in these negotiations. The credibility of national redemocratization regimes, as in Brazil or Argentina, or of long-standing political coalitions, as in Mexico, may play a role in the outcome—if not in some either-or sense, at least in working out the details. (And, of course, as the New York case also suggests, national cohesion may involve foregoing some more militant options, so it is not an option to be undertaken uncritically or lightly by participants.)

Managing Retrenchment

When New York began to respond to the fiscal crisis, a number of observers saw the possibility of putting city government on a more efficient basis. E.S. Savas (1975) saw the crisis as a "Golden Opportunity to close the budget gap... and to prove that New York is indeed manageable." By this he presumably meant it afforded an opportunity to end services and subsidies that conservatives saw as unnecessary, and to weaken union power, as well as to streamline the delivery of desired services. A good many liberals would have shared at least the latter hope. Many radical critics, like Lichten, suggest, of course, that breaking unions and disenfranchising the poor was a more important aim, but another major radical scholar, Francis Fox Piven, suggested at the time that "a kind of bureaucratic politics has prevailed." In her view the weakest elements of the agencies were lopped off, but in a chaotic, rather than a planned way (Piven, 1976).

The observation of actual cutbacks in the immediate crisis period, and over the subsequent decade, suggests that each of these views has part of the truth. The unions were not destroyed, but they were forced in a direction of collaboration rather than militance. Services to the poor were indeed cut, with disastrous results in some cases, but the pattern of cutbacks was not as tightly and uniformly regressive as might have been feared. The middle class also suffered severe losses of services. And while some services may have been streamlined and made more efficient, many were disrupted and made less efficient.

A first approximation to the effects of cuts can be seen in actual city budget and employment data. Table 2 shows changes in the city budget. Table 3 shows employment figures, as estimated in the mayors' annual budget messages. A direct before and after comparison is difficult, because a number of employees,

Table 2

New York City Expense Budget (Billions of Dollars)

		1973-1974 Actual	1977-1978 Mayor's Proposal	1985-1986 Proposal
Incomes				
	State and Federal Aid	4.5 B$	5.1 B$	7.2 B$
	Property taxes	2.7	3.2	4.4
	Other revenues (taxes, fees and, for 1973-1974, short term borrowing).	3.0	5.6	8.4
	Total Income	10.2 B$	13.9 B$	20.0 B$
Expenses				
	Debt Service	1.1 B$	1.9 B$	1.4 B$
	Welfare, Human Resources	2.9	3.3	4.8
	Education	2.3	3.4	4.2
	Police and Fire	1.0	1.3	3.4*
	Health	0.9	1.0	1.0
	Other	2.0	3.0	5.2
	Total	10.2 B$	13.9 B$	20.0 B$
	Total except for debt service	9.1 B$	12.0 B$	18.6 B$
Consumer Price Index		133	181	322

(*Includes other aspects of administration of justice). Source: New York Times.

Table 3

New York City Agency Reductions (Number of Employees)

Department	12/31/74	6/30/75	8/31/75	6/30/76	6/30/84
Education (Bd. of Ed.)	79,852	90,182	71,072	76,782	73,949
Police	35,411	35,734	31,096	30,842	29,707
Fire	14,003	13,921	12,454	12,181	13,470
Social Services	26,768	27,122	23,822	24,364	22,278
EPA (Sanitation)	19,074	19,072	16,596	16,451	15,779
Total (Includes other city agencies)	294,522	254,400	258,635	218,463	201,280

Source: New York Times (11-12-75 and 5-4-85), PSC Clarion (9-1-76), citing data from New York City Office of Management and Budget. Figures not fully consistent as to whether part-time workers are included.

such as those in City University senior colleges and in city hospitals, were transferred from the city payroll to "autonomous" or state-government agencies. Nonetheless, the presence of many cuts is clear. The figures show that cuts came rapidly in 1975, and have been minor since 1976. Cuts have been shallower in the uniformed services and education than in other areas. But no service is untouched.

These gross figures do not tell the story of efficiency changes or the inter-community or internal distribution of cuts within agencies. Information on these matters is available from a survey performed by Queens College students at the time of the initial and deepest cuts; from a series of annual conferences on "Setting Municipal Priorities" (Brecher and Horton, 1983) and from other specific studies and press reports (as well as the author's own observations as a city resident).

The student survey, taken only a year into the retrenchment process, showed a pattern of nearly-random and often irrational cuts. In the Police Department, the most visible of city agencies, varying announcements of larger and smaller numbers of cuts were made; precinct closings were ordered and rescinded; programs and units such as traffic control, community relations, mounted and emergency rescue, harbor and aviation patrols, and campaigns against prostitution, gambling, pornography and narcotics were threatened with closure. Many of the announced cuts were only threats designed to protect the department by ensuring public opposition. Although opposition prevented closing of precincts or programs, many remained operating with only skeleton staffs. In the process, programs were disrupted and many officers were laid off and rehired again at different times. Morale fell to a very low level.

In general the department tried to maintain the visibility of uniformed men, so that the number of undercover or plain clothes staff fell. One of the major controversies concerned the use of one-man rather than two-man patrol cars, in the city's lower-density areas. These cuts were resisted as unsafe by the patrolmen's union, but were finally imposed, to a limited extent, in return for avoiding some other cuts. This was supposed to maintain patrol car coverage in the face of manpower cuts. But for the first several years of the crisis, the change did not have this effect. Because auto repair personnel had been judged less essential than patrolmen, patrol car maintenance fell behind, so that vehicles rather than patrolmen were the limiting factor. In one precinct surveyed, lack of cars was keeping most officers to foot duty near the stationhouse, so that despite little loss of staff, the district perceived a loss of protection.

Similar problems befell the Board of Education. Cuts in school personnel led to more crowded classes, a predictable result of any cuts. But further disruption was found to occur because, with cuts going on, and a complex seniority system in effect, teachers might be moved from class to class, or school to school, many times in a year. Classes could have four or five teachers during the year, as funds came and went, or as errors in seniority preference were corrected. Meanwhile, the bureaus assigned to run tests for new teachers managed to avoid major cuts, even though for several years there were no new teachers to test.

In the social service agencies, cuts reflected a sense of these services as less essential than the uniformed service, and the general powerlessness of poor clients. Foster care, daycare and other human resource programs were cut, often drastically, saving money on their specific budgets. But the result was often just to shift cases, often to higher cost services, as lack of home care drove people into hospitals or nursing homes. The welfare program itself, which was mandated by federal and state laws, could only cut its grant expenditures by stricter enforcement of eligibility standards. But this was foiled by the system's own budget cutting, as record keeping and enforcement fell further behind. The main force holding rolls down became delay in processing the intake of new cases, but this in turn would have a drastic effect on city expenditures over the next decade, by contributing to the inability of the city to fend off the rise of homelessness among welfare families. (Only a decade later did the city's Human Resources Administration try to design an early warning system to determine which welfare families might face eviction and homelessness.)

A number of agencies have done somewhat better at making service provision more efficient. The Fire Department and the Department of Sanitation both eventually managed to win acclaim for greater efficiency. But both departments already had been undergoing major professional studies of possible efficiencies when the crisis began, and in the case of the Fire Department, a strong sense of the department's importance kept morale high. Nonetheless, in the early years of the crisis, even these departments faced problems.

The Fire Department reduced crew sizes and removed some vehicles, lengthening the average response time slightly (with some resulting increase in the fires that became serious structural fires). A reduction in fire inspections made problems worse. In this situation, firemen were exhorted by management to think positively, to emphasize the positive side of the job, and to stress their accomplishments. It was felt that by highlighting heroic deeds and dedication, arguments against further cuts would be reinforced. However, doing a good job in the face of cuts could also create the perception that a larger staff was not needed. The Department responded by giving heavy publicity to the problem of arson in the South Bronx and other decaying areas, thereby demonstrating the need for their services. But this also spread a sense of fear; by highlighting flight and disinvestment, it may have increased the arson problem.

In the case of sanitation, morale was greatly reduced by the initial round of cuts. These made pickups less frequent, without of course affecting the actual tonnage of garbage to be moved. Hence, at times, crews required expensive overtime, while neighborhoods were angered at the delays and the eventual nighttime pickups. A press campaign against "lazy" workers was an added irritant.

It is not surprising that while Fire Department morale remained high, sanitation workers staged a brief summer strike to remind the city of their importance. In the end, new and more efficient trucks were introduced, reducing crew needs and speeding pickups somewhat. But the decade of attention to the pickup function had deflected attention from the more serious problem of where to put the garbage. This was reaching crisis proportions due to the exhaustion of landfill sites, and now needs urgent attention.

Some Specific Lessons

These and other examples of initial or continuing troubles and/or occasional eventual success stories of efficiency suggest several things about the management of retrenchment, which will undoubtedly be faced by Latin American city and central governments as well. These might be ameliorated (although not entirely avoided) by attention to the New York lesson.

The first is the simple fact that speed in cutbacks, while it responds to creditor demands and may help to spread the sense of crisis, precludes careful planning and can only lead to irrationalities like one-manning the absent police cars. Patterns of shunting cases from one service to another may mean that service costs, in the end, do not decline, despite specific cutbacks.

Second, New York exhibits a tendency to cut, when possible, by delaying or ending maintenance expenditures on equipment, as a way of avoiding immediate service cuts. New York also shows how wasteful this tendency may be. Immediate service disruption from maintenance cuts, as in the case of New York's patrol cars, may be unusual. But over the subsequent ten years, the difficulties engendered by undermaintenance of road and transit systems, and numerous other facilities, have become clear. In the New York case, the maintenance problem had begun a few years before the fiscal crisis fully emerged, as the availability of bond-financed capital spending money outstripped funds for maintenance from tax-levy budgets. The crisis made it worse and the eventual result was near-disaster. The city faces high replacement costs.

Third, New York suggests that planning for a more rational, long-term retrenchment is difficult. One reason is technical. Cutbacks in personnel or in rates of facility utilization are easy to make. Closing of facilities is, however, often an irreversible decision: restarting costs may be high or infinite, and the closing of facilities may lead to other forms of disinvestment in an area (Wolpert and Seley, 1986). Thus rational planning for facility consolidation is difficult in the presence of any uncertainty about future turnaround or continuance of trends. The second reason is institutional: with each agency trying to protect its own services, and with most planning done at the agency level, the central authority must make its plans on the basis of limited and fundamentally flawed information. The third reason is political: any cuts lead to opposition, and government must balance competing claims. In the New York case, pressures prevented as much service cutback as there was population decline in areas of decay (although they did not prevent regressivity altogether) but it is unclear whether this was "rational" or not. Dolan, Wolpert and Seley's (1986) allocation matrix, which they suggest might have been used for more rational cutting, is based on explicitly limited assumptions.

Fourth, a neglected set of problems that emerges with cuts or with interrupted growth concerns the "demographic pyramid" within agencies. In an agency that is either growing slowly or stable in size, there is likely to be a stable relationship between the number of young employees and the slightly lower number of older ones. This allows for supervision and initiation of new employees by older ones, and for some reasonable hope of advancement to higher-level positions. Recruits assume that at least some of their cohorts will advance as the top of the "pyramid" retires. In some cases of very rapid growth of an organization, younger recruits greatly outnumber older staff and some may have to advance "prematurely" into management, but their resulting problems of inexperience may at least be balanced by the élan of progress. But in the aftermath of retrenchment, there will be other problems. An end to recruiting, and firings of those with low seniority, leads to a staff with most members concentrated in the somewhat older age group: a diamond, not a pyramid.

The lack of younger staff may itself cause problems. The Fire Department feared for a time its staff might not have the vigor needed, although in the end this proved less of a problem than expected. The City University, with a more sedentary staff, might seem less troubled. But it now finds itself with a faculty mostly in the senior ranks and largely tenured, who in some units are suffering a sense of middle aged burnout and have trouble communicating with younger students. The traffic department, with a small and highly specialized staff, had an imbalance between staff skills and needs after it made its cuts on the basis of seniority.

Nor do the problems end when the aging staff is finally replaced. In the Police Department, where a lower age for voluntary retirement means that the cohort of budget-cut survivors is now retiring, and where some expansion is again occuring, a large new cohort of recruits finds there are few experienced lower-middle-rank colleagues to socialize them into department traditions. This has been suggested as one partial reason for publicized indiscipline in such areas as prisoner treatment and use of excessive force.

Finally, all of these irrationalities suggest a deeper problem, which can arise in any system in the absence of very high solidarity and which is particularly acute where a market system leaves unemployment and individual economic privation as a real threat. That is that the scramble of individuals and groups to preserve their own short-term viability (in every sense) will lead to conflict, competition, withholding of information, political maneuvering, and a general war of all against all: union vs. union, service vs. service, neighborhood vs. neighborhood, ethnic group vs. ethnic group, and individual vs. individual. Worst, this will occur just when social solidarity is needed to confront the crisis.

V
New York as a Third World City?

The changes in New York since the outset of fiscal crisis suggest one other parallel with Latin America, and one other image for New York. In recent years, many observers have made casual suggestions that New York is becoming more like Third World cities. Widening income and consumption disparities, visible homelessness and informal economic activity, and deteriorating public service quality all suggest the comparison (Franco, 1985).

The analogy is not without its dangers. If New York's problems are seen as "Third Worldization," they may be blamed unfairly on Third World immigrants. If New York complains of Third World problems despite its wealth, this may denigrate the problems of poorer cities. Nonetheless, there is probably something to the view that parallels have arisen between New York and

Latin American or Third World Cities. It becomes harder to see "modern" and "underdeveloped" cities as entirely different in their functioning. (On the problems of a simple "modern-nonmodern" dichotomy see Edel, 1988.)

Determining how valid or widely applicable the parallels are requires systematic analysis, rather than just casual observation. A preliminary analysis has been attempted by a symposium on "New York as a Third World City," held as part of the Bildner Center's Urban Challenge Project. This forum suggested several approaches to examining the parallels. The main speakers, John Mollenkopf, Saskia Sassen-Koob, Ximena de la Barra and Matthew Edel, suggested several areas of difference and similarity between New York and Third World Cities. Differences were cited in living standards, in rates of growth, in centrality as nodes in a world financial hierarchy, in cosmopolitan heterogeneity and in the infrastructure for housing and services. Similarities or resemblances included the increasing importance of cities as nodes in a linked world communication, financial and political system; their decreasing role as housing industrial centers (deindustrialization was cited in Santiago and other Latin American cities, as well as in U.S. cities); the shrinkage of the middle class and the increase of mass poverty in elite space; an increase in the scope and magnitude of immigration, even in the absence of net population growth; and an increasing presence of "informal" or "underground" economic activities. (These last extend from official corruption and business avoidance of taxes, unions and regulations; through multiple job holding by the middle class and the proliferation of "informal" small businesses in commerce and manufacturing; to informal housing arrangements and employment for the poor.) In addition, certain problems seen previously as "developed nation" urban ills, such as the inadequate coordination of cities and suburbs, or the externalities of pollution and congestion, have also spread to the Third World.

Looking at these phenomena, Mollenkopf and de la Barra suggested the question was not whether New York was "like" Third World cities, but whether there was convergence of certain key traits. If likeness is measured on an array of characteristics, the panelists agreed, similarities were increasing although differences remained.

This arraying of characteristics is not, however, a complete theoretical framework. Sassen-Koob suggested a distinction between empirical patterns observed, and underlying processes that generated these patterns (as well as between both of these, and theoretical formulations about these processes). She suggested that similar outcomes might be generated by different processes.

Effort is still needed to elucidate these processes. Sassen-Koob suggested that two theoretical processes might have to be considered: the core-periphery notion, and the notion of a world economic system itself subject to trends and cycles. The interaction of these two might be studied.

In a simple core-periphery model, New York becoming more "like" Third World cities might mean that the U.S. was losing position relative to other nations which were moving up in position. This does not seem to be the central cause of observed similarities, however. Rather, changes in the world economy seem to be raising, at least for the moment, the importance of financial node activities in major cities. Meanwhile, increasing trade and migration are intensifying inter-place competition in manufacturing and exportable services, and hence pressing downward on working class and middle class living standards. This in turn causes parallel income distribution and land use changes in cities at all levels of center and periphery. Resemblance in informalization, migration and poverty result. As cities themselves have to compete for investment and government resources services are pressured by fiscal crisis. Finally, all areas feel the pinch of a "long-swing" slowdown in the world economy (see Edel 1976, Gordon 1978, Harvey 1982).

These similarities may intercut with and override differences stemming from the center-periphery distinction, or they may modify them. One major distinction between center and periphery has been the degree to which the center has used "autocentric, articulated" growth strategies supported by and supporting an implicit interclass social compromise, while the periphery has not. (see Amin 1979, de Janvry 1981, Przeworski 1985). If present trends or cycles in the world economy are weakening this articulation in the "centers" (at least insofar as civilian consumption is important as an element in autocentric growth), then the increasing similarity of urban phenomena may indeed relate to a change in the very nature of center-periphery differences.

To determine the extent of these possible underlying tendencies, and their link to the convergence of some urban phenomena, will require much more analysis than can be attempted here. But a tentative conclusion can be presented: in several dimensions New York's resemblances to Latin American cities have increased.

These resemblances may point to increasing similarities between the economic structures of center and periphery, and to the roles of cities there. Whatever they mean about macro-societal trends, the similarities suggest new possibilities that North American and Latin American cities can learn from each others' experiences.

References

Albion, Robert. *Rise of The New York Port.* Evanston: Northwestern University Press, 1984.

Alcaly R. and Mermelstein, D. *The Fiscal Crisis of American Cities.* New York: Vintage, 1976.

Amin, Samir. *Unequal Development.* New York: Monthly Review Press, 1976.

Auletta, Ken. *The Streets Were Paved with Gold.* New York: Vintage, 1980.

Bailey, Robert W. *The Crisis Regime.* Albany: State University of New York Press, 1985.

Bowles, S., Gordon D. and Weisskopf, T. *Beyond the Wasteland.* New York: Doubleday, 1983.

Brecher, Charles and Horton, Ray. *Setting Municipal Priorities 1982.* New York: New York University Press, 1983.

DeJanvry, Alain. *The Agrarian Question and Reformism in Latin America.* Baltimore: Johns Hopkins University Press, 1981.

DeKadt, M., Hoffman J. and Edel, M. "Business's Plans for New York." *Social Policy,* May-June 1981, 7-15.

Dolan, L.W., Wolpert, J., and Seley, J.E. "Dynamic Municipal Allocation Analysis," *Environment and Planning A* (1986)

Edel, Matthew. "The New York Crisis as Economic History," in Alcaly, R. and Mermelstein D,. *The Fiscal Crisis of American Cities.* New York: Vintage Books, 1976.

—"Latin American Cities: Recognizing Complexities," *Latin American Research Review.* XXIII: 1, 165-174, 1988.

Edel, M., Sclar, E. and Luria, D. *Shaky Palaces.* New York: Columbia University Press, 1984.

Editors of Fortune, *The Exploding Metropolis.* Garden City: Anchor, 1958.

Feretti, Fred. *The Year the Big Apple Went Bust.* New York: Putnam, 1976.

Fitch, Robert. "Planning New York," in R. Alcaly and D. Mermelstein, eds., *The Fiscal Crisis of American Cities.* New York: Vintage Books, 1976.

Franco, Jean. "New York is a Third-World City," *Tabloid:* A Review of Mass Culture and Everyday Life, 9 (1985), 12-31.

Gordon, David. "Capitalist Development and the History of American Cities," in W. K. Tabb and L. Sawers, *Marxism and the Metropolis.* New York: Oxford University Press, 1978.

—"Up and Down The Long Roller Coaster," in Union for Radical Political Economics, eds., *U. S. Capitalism in Crisis.* New York: URPE, 1973.

Hall, Peter. *The World Cities.* New York: McGraw Hill, 1966.

Harvey, David. *The Limits to Capital.* Chicago: University of Chicago Press, 1982.

Hoover, E.M. and Vernon, Raymond. *Anatomy of a Metropolis.* Cambridge: Harvard University Press, 1959.

Koch, Edward. *Mayor.* New York: Simon and Schuster, 1984.

Kouwenhoven, John, A. *The Columbia Historical Portrait of New York.* New York: Doubleday, 1953.

Lichten, Eric. *Class, Power and Austerity: The New York City Fiscal Crisis.* South Hadley, Mass.: Bergin and Garvey, 1986.

Mollenkopf, J., de la Barra, X., Edel, M., and Sassen-Koob, S., "Panel Discussion: Is New York Becoming More Like a Third World City," Summary document, Bildner Center for Western Hemisphere Studies, 1985.

Morris, Charles R. *The Cost of Good Intentions.* New York: McGraw Hill, 1980.

Newfield, Jack and DuBruhl, Paul. *The Abuse of Power.* New York: Penguin, 1978.

O'Connor, James. *The Fiscal Crisis of The State.* New York: St. Martins Press, 1973.

Piven, Francis Fox. "Slicing the Big Apple," *Liberation* . Spring, 1976.

Przeworski, Adam. *Capitalism and Social Democracy.* Cambridge: Cambridge University Press, 1985.

Robertson, Wyndam. "Going Broke the New York Way." *Fortune.* August, 1975. Pp. 144, et. seq.

Sassen-Koob, Saskia. "The New Labor Demand in Global Cities," in Michael P. Smith, ed. *Cities in Transformation.* Beverly Hills, California: Sage Publications, 1984. Pp. 139-171.

Savas, E. S. "The Budget Gap and the Performance Gap," *New York Affairs,* 3:1, Fall, 1975, 112-119.

Starr, Roger. *The Rise and Fall of New York City.* New York: Basic Books, 1985.

Tabb, William. "Blaming the Victim," in L. Sawers and W. Tabb, eds., *Marxism and The Metropolis.* New York: Oxford University Press.

—*The Long Default.* New York: Monthly Review Press, 1982.

Temporary Commission on City Finances. *The City in Crisis.* New York: Arno Press, 1978.

Wolpert, Julian and Seley, John. "Urban Neighborhoods as a National Resource: Irreversible Decisions and their Equity Spillovers," *Geographical Analysis,* 18:1 (Jan. 1986), 81-93.

5 Buenos Aires: Class Structure, Public Policy and the Urban Poor

by Elizabeth Jelin

This paper discusses some recent developments in the urban scene of the city of Buenos Aires, related to the policies of the military dictatorship that ruled the country during the period 1976-1983, and the more recent effects of the democratization process.

Government Policy and the Urban Background

Buenos Aires is a large city and it has been so for a very long time. The population of the metropolitan area, according to the 1980 Census, is almost ten million people (9,700,000). Buenos Aires is an old city: the Federal District (that is, the central part of the city) grew in the latter part of the nineteenth century and in the early twentieth century; then again after the Second World War. But the core city did not grow significantly from 1950 to 1980. From 1970 to 1980, the Federal District actually decreased by 2.2% in population. By 1980 it had nearly 3,000,000 people. The surrounding area of the city, Greater Buenos Aires, which administratively is part of the Province of Buenos Aires, grew from 1970 to 1980 by 27%, reaching a population of 6,800,000. In other words, during the ten-year period from 1970 to 1980 there was a very important reshuffling of the population of the city: not so much population growth as a process of change in the internal distribution of its population.

The difference between the central city and the surrounding areas is very important. The supply of public services is greatly different in one and in the other. In the city, there is a considerable supply of services, with an old but still functioning network of water supply, public transportation, paved streets, electricity and sewage. The surrounding areas are much more heterogeneous in this regard.

From 1970 to 1980 there was increasing suburbanization. The areas near the central city grew the least; those further away grew most. The new population coming to the city had to search for housing quite far into the suburbs; also, many residents of the center city had to move further out into the suburbs.

This movement was the result, in part, of an explicit and clear governmental policy: the military coup of March 1976 was an attempt to produce structural alterations of the Argentine economy, society and polity. Based on a diagnosis of social, economic and political illness and chaos, the Armed Forces proposed deep changes geared to restore order. The means to be used varied: open repression, a freeze on political and trade-union activities, strict control and indirect censorship of information and cultural life, and a large list of economic policies designed to reestablish order and discipline (Canitrot, 1981).

Rather than reporting the whole spectrum of policies of the dictatorship and their effects on the society, let me look at those that affected mostly the popular sectors. From the vantage point of the organization of daily life of urban working-class families, the dimensions of public policy and of the performance of the economy that are relevant were: a) the conditions of the labor market: b) inflation and shifts in relative prices of consumer goods; and c) the supply of public services and urban policies.

With regard to the labor market, the neo-liberal economic team that was in charge after the 1976 coup faced one important restriction to its plan: the military banned any drastic increase in unemployment, in clear contrast to the situation in Chile after 1973. The Argentine military could not accept an increase in unemployment, fearing that such a condition would generate unrest and popular protest movements. In fact, during the period 1976-1979 there was almost full employment in Argentina.

Wage levels were a different matter: one of the first economic measures after the 1976 coup was a nominal-wage freeze. Given the high rate of inflation, this meant a considerable and sudden decline in real wages (of more than 30% in three months). This was accompanied, as said above, by a relatively favorable labor market. Although industrial employment declined, the displaced workers were absorbed by other sectors, especially as self-employed workers in services (Beccaria and Orsatti, 1985). Meanwhile, after the first "shock" of early 1976, wages maintained their relative low level, with a slight increase during 1980-1981, to fall again in 1982. By 1981, the economic and political crisis had reached a point at which open unemployment increased considerably, thus altering one of the basic conditions of the military government.

A second important dimension was the unequaled rate of inflation of the Argentine economy during the previous several years. Since not all prices shifted at the same time, there were drastic changes in relative prices of consumer goods. Prices changed suddenly and in jumps, making it impossible to predict and plan budgets and expenses. Under such conditions, uncertainty becomes endemic in the social fabric of everyday life.

The third dimension was the decline in the supply of public services. This policy was based on the belief that a great part of the problem with Argentine society had to do with the fact that the labor movement had too much power and that it was too much of a state-oriented society. The cure would come from restoring a society where the free market could operate. This implied a drastic change in government action toward the subordinate classes, including the shift to the marketplace or privatization of services that were defined previously as state-provided, or even as citizenship rights. Some of the public services—health, for instance—were already in poor shape and declining before the military came to power. The military's policy gave them a final blow.

In the area of health, several national hospitals were closed. A new system of fees was instituted, to be paid by the public for health care in public hospitals, which could be avoided through a complex bureaucratic mechanism to obtain a "certificate of indigency." Physicians and nurses used to the previous open-door policy of public hospitals found ways to circumvent official instructions and still, with a humanitarian ideology, deliver services without bureaucratic red tape. But it was not easy, and not all of them were ready to run the risks involved at a time when repression and control were the rule (Llovet, 1984).

There was also a policy of decentralization and transfer of public services from the central to the provincial and municipal governments. That meant a decline in the services offered by national hospitals and their replacement by the existing municipal ones. For the Metropolitan Area of Buenos Aires, which administratively is divided between the Federal District and the province of Buenos Aires (including 19 municipalities), it implied a decline in the services that the poorer people of the outskirts could get: the better-equipped hospitals of the capital were not available to residents of the province any more. Each administrative unit had to serve its own population, rather than being able to use whatever service was available in the Metropolitan Area.

Up to that time, a very large proportion of the population had received health services through labor union clinics and *Obras Sociales*. Unions either had their own hospitals or contracted with private clinics. In order to decrease the power of the unions, the government took away from them the handling of their health system, since it involved, of course, managing very large financial resources.

Other services were also affected. Public transportation was traditionally a subsidized service. Subsidies of various sorts disappeared, thus increasing costs considerably, at a time when distances to and from work increased, given the geographical relocation of the poorer sectors of the population. Of course, the educational system was also affected by the policies of decentralization and privatization, although the impact was more clearly on quality of the educational services than on attendance statistics (Tedesco, Braslavsky and Carciofi, 1983).

In the area of housing and urban relocation, three specific policies had great impact. First was removal of squatter settlements in the central city. Many of the settlers in these areas were immigrants from Paraguay and Bolivia or internal migrants from the poorer provinces. Those who could show that they owned a lot somewhere in the suburbs could stay in the Metropolitan Area. Others were forced to go back to their places of origin. The only strategy of the population to resist forced emigration was to buy some relatively cheap and distant small lot (many times jointly with others) and move there when their settlement was dismantled; or else preventively to move in with relatives, thus increasing overcrowding. This explains in part the growth of the out-of-the-way suburbs: areas 25 miles out of the city where infrastructural services are minimal, and where land speculation is the basic criterion for land development.

Second was repeal of rent control. Rent controls had existed in Argentina for many years. Some of the rent freezes went back to the 1940s, and thus many people lived in very run-down buildings, similar to the poorest tenements of New York City. But still they were in the city, and paid almost no rent. As part of the policy of the military regime, rents were left open to market forces. The poor tenants were evicted, to allow restoration of old buildings for commercial and/or middle class residential use.

Third, the program of urban highway construction also implied the forced move of poor urban dwellers (Oszlak, 1983).

The end result, as tourists coming to the city at that time could testify, was the city that the military wanted to show to the world during the Soccer World Cup in 1978: a clean, beautiful city, with tree-lined streets, with parks and flowers, blooming bushes and efficient traffic. It is a beautiful place to be: middle class, safe, with no poor people around.

On a broader political and ideological level, the exclusion of all channels of expression of dissent and the prevalence of fear led to increased uncertainty, not only in economic terms, but also in personal and family life. Longer-term personal and family plans did not disappear, but they were postponed. The forefront of everyday life was taken over by more immediate issues, the "drama" of surviving. At the same time, the government committed itself to a major ideological operation, the "change of mentalities," intended to destroy collective identities and to replace them by the marketplace—the impersonal arena where individuals (never collectivities) exchange their goods and services—as the basic mechanism of social life.

At a time when political repression was at its height, and fear was the basic motivation in life, no popular or social movement of protest against any of these policies emerged. The outcries were minimal, and there was no available information on what was going on on a daily basis: a squatter settlement could be erased by bulldozers one day, with no reporting of it in mass media. No journalist dared to report on such things.

Everyday Life Among the Urban Subordinate Sector: A Research Project

In 1979, at a time when political repression and fear were at their height, we began a longitudinal study of everyday life of a small number of urban families on a qualitative basis, to be able to reconstruct what was going on during the military dictatorship. The study was based on in-depth interviews and participant observation of a set of low-income households in Greater Buenos Aires, visited frequently during a three-year period (1979-1982). All adults and adolescent members of the households were interviewed repeatedly, and these interviews were complemented by the observation of household activities under a variety of circumstances. Most interviews were tape-recorded, and although there were thematic guidelines in most cases, the interviews were very open and often did not follow the format the researcher had in mind. Whenever it was relevant, the respondent's own views, criteria and discourse took precedence over the systematic recording based on analytically developed categories and questions. Given the character of the study, focused on daily activities and household organization, the main respondents, with whom rapport was established and maintained all along the period of field-work, were the women in charge of the domestic tasks.[1]

This was not a neighborhood or community study; the families were scattered all around the city. There were two reasons for that: first and foremost, fear. We thought it would have been much more suspicious and dangerous, for ourselves and for the families we were studying, to be a visible and active presence in one specific neighborhood day in and day out. Second, we were certain that coping mechanisms in everyday life were at that time basically at the family and informal network basis; community activities were at their historical lowest.

The aim of the study was to analyze how families construct their ways of life and level of living, looking at the market and non-market forces to which they had to adapt, since families could do almost nothing to change these conditions. Three basic dimensions of well-being were studied in detail: patterns of work, the allocation of resources—both monetary and non-monetary—and consumption patterns. The consumption dimension includes not only purchased goods but especially collective consumption patterns, of great relevance because of the political meanings of public goods in Argentina.

The Peronist tradition was anchored in the relationship between the popular sectors and the state as a provider of public services. Although it had a class base, Peronism was not class-politics. Rather, popular support was based on broadening the dimensions of social citizenship, through an appeal to social justice. One of the long-term effects of Peronist rule during the 1940s and early 1950s has been on social relations in everyday life. A slogan of that time, *Perón cumple, Evita dignifica* (Peron fulfills, Evita dignifies) symbolizes this image. This sense of dignity is highly relevant in Argentine society. During several decades, the symbolic dimension of the collective identity of the popular sectors in Argentina has been linked to the idea of dignity—and dignity implies, in practical terms, broadening social citizenship rights through collective consumption. Dignity means being a citizen; being a citizen means having access to state services. At the present, that symbolic dimension is to a large extent in crisis.

When these social services break down, when the military dictatorship cuts these services, it is not only material life that deteriorates; the sense of self and dignity is also under attack. Although the relative standard of living of the Argentine working-class population during the dictatorship might not have been lower than in other Latin American countries, given the historical gains of the working class, comparisons should not be made on the "objective" indicators of well-being in a static way, but rather in terms of the changes over time and especially in terms of their meanings to the people themselves. The meaning of an unsatisfied need is very different when it has not been incorporated as part of the rights that are taken for granted, or when it is part of the rights that are being attacked and repressed.

Thus, well-being is a rather complex concept that includes monetary income and other transfers based on informal networks and on state and union services. It also includes the dimension of the understanding and the significance of a certain pattern of life for the actors themselves. Even in cases where monetary income was not declining, the sense of uncertainty and arbitrariness was very powerful: uncertainty was linked to inflation, to randomness at times of repression, to unpredictability in social services: what will I be able to buy tomorrow with the money I have? Will I come back safely when I go to work? Will I find everything as usual at home? Will I get attention in a hospital if my child is sick?

Let me illustrate everyday life of the popular sector with some examples of consumption patterns.

Any observer concerned with living standards of popular sectors from a "rational" perspective based on "real" consumption needs, giving priority to health and a better allocation of present and future work, would be horrified when visiting some urban Argentine families during the early 1980s. Hi-fi systems (often broken) in houses with no glass windows, a color television set in a house with no running water, were not uncommon sights. If some administratively defined criterion of well-being based on a "scientifically" determined hierarchy of needs were to be taken, one would be astonished by the degree of overconsumption of appliances in relation to other goods and services, especially the quality of housing. The fashionable clothes of adolescents would also be noticeable.

Access to housing on the part of popular sectors is difficult (Feijoo, 1983). Costs are high and not easily included in the regular budget of a working-class family. The "big" decisions imply obligations for many years: the plot of land that is paid in unending installments, the house that is constructed little by little, enlarging, improving, being lived in, always half-finished. Construction materials are purchased when money is available, and accumulated slowly until the day the addition of a room or other improvements can be completed. These projects develop in waves: small quantities of goods are accumulated, or money is saved, until a threshold is reached and construction of a new room begins. Its implications are months, if not years, of debts, in addition to the slow process of work to finish the project—often totally or partially based on self-construction and help from informal networks.

Domestic furnishings are another story. Living spaces are small, furniture tends to be old, broken, second-hand purchases or hand-me-downs from relatives. Electric appliances, on the other hand, were numerous and were almost constantly being purchased, adding to and renewing the domestic stock.

These goods are acquired solely through purchase, rather than by loan or transfers through informal networks. Neither are they part of those public goods and services that can be received by "right" or through charity. That is, these are privately acquired goods for family use. Each one of these appliances has, without doubt, a certain use-value which contributes to family well-being, be it saving domestic labor (refrigerators, washing machines), adding to the level of information or contributing to recreation (television, record player, tape recorder). This use-value influences the decision to purchase the good. But there are additional factors that explain their massive presence in the popular sector homes during the dictatorship.

From 1976 to 1980, with the free-trade policy and the opening-up of the economy, the market was flooded with imported electrical appliances, including products that were new to Argentine consumption (hi-fi and color TV). Families of the popular sectors were active buyers in this market. The deep recession of the 1980s and more recent changes in economic policy have led to a severe decline in the sales of this type of product, and eventually to the impossibility of repairing the old ones or replacing them when they break down.

Electrical appliances were bought because the supply was there, aggressively attacking the potential consumer, offering credit and flexible payment conditions, apparently adequate for any family. Usually, families have established credit in a neighborhood appliance store. This is not the impersonal credit of large department stores, but a relationship in which personal acquaintance plays a crucial role. The loan appears to be constantly active, renewed as soon as the debt for the previously purchased object is going to be paid off. The merchant seems to maintain an inventory of the goods each family-client already has, and what it "could" want or need, displaying these goods to generate the need and the demand. For example, one of the interviewed families began to talk about cassette players, including references to the recording equipment used in the interviews; within a few months, the cassette recorder was on the table. Shortly afterward, the conversation began to include the advantages of color TV. A brochure on color TV was provided by the merchant-friend when they went to pay the installment on the record player. No more than a few months elapsed before the color television set entered the family gatherings.

The objects are not always useful or usable. A floor polisher given as a gift for Mother's Day stands in the corner of a room for two years, without ever being used because it is entirely inappropriate for cement floors. It was bought in the hope that the floor will be improved and waxing might then begin. In another case, the broken record player, being so large, takes up a very large share of the limited living space of a family with ten children. Furthermore, the appliances break easily, given that the instructions for their use are not simple and often the electrical wiring in the houses is totally inadequate. And if the monthly installment is part of the current budget (sometimes overdue a few days or even a month, but not much more given the danger of repossession by the seller with a loss of whatever had already been paid), this is not the case with expenses linked to repairs. These are unpredictable and can seldom be done when the appliance is out of order. The number of broken appliances waiting for months to be repaired in working-class homes is enormous.

Similarly, in clothing, the contrast observed between different family members is enormous. Without any doubt, adolescents are the best dressed. Not only is their clothing in good condition and clean, but it always follows the latest fashion. Clothing for teenagers is a subject of permanent discussion and decision in the family circle. The adolescents plead, demand. It is not that they directly control the money, but they demand from their parents who, with a greater or lesser degree of acceptance, finally concede to pressure.

Why do parents give in so much? It is clear that there are altruistic feelings on the part of the parents, who feel satisfaction when they see their children happy. It is also true that the media orient their messages to the young, conscious of their influence on decisions on family expenditures. But the family interaction around these subjects includes more than the parents giving in to pressure. It appears to reflect the acceptance of adolescent fashionable clothing as a *need*. The same is true for the cash to go out with friends, dancing, to a cafe, or to attend the concert of a popular singer.

What symbolic value do these objects have for families of the popular sector? Why do they buy them? Both in the case of electric appliances and in adolescent leisure time consumption, a mechanism of "public presentation" of the family is functioning. In relation to electrical appliances, given the impossibility of ever acquiring more adequate housing and the very high costs of home improvements, there is emphasis on owning the more accessible consumer goods. These are the newest, stylish objects that can be displayed or that can help in building a more acceptable family image, not only in social relations that take place inside the home environment but even outside, in the public sphere. The possibility of making comments on color TV or on the newest cassette refers to a field of positive definition of social identities. In fact, it allows seeing oneself as integrated into the world of consumption and not as a marginal social being.

Furthermore, it is basically the aspirations and desires of the young that are taken into account (Jelin, 1984). The adolescents are the ones who participate most in commercial leisure activities, who go out the most, who have the most contacts outside kinship circles (except, of course, those contacts related to the work situation). That a son or a daughter should "have nothing to put on" or not to be able to go dancing for lack of money would be a pointedly obvious manifestation of failure, not only of the young, but of their parents who cannot provide what they need. In the case of appliances, the normal Argentine working-class family has for several decades been able to acquire the basic home appliances (refrigerators, gas stoves, radios, sewing machines). What has been added in the last decade are goods tied to leisure time of the young. In a certain sense, access to these new consumer goods, which until recently were seen as "luxuries" for the rich, has functioned as a mechanism to compensate for (or hide) the deterioration of public services such as health or education and of the general level of well-being.

To summarize, electrical appliances and clothes for the young are "overloaded" with meanings. At a time when social rights were being repressed, when channels of participation were closed, when income and services were on the decline, the ability of a popular sector household to purchase these goods was evidence that their living conditions were not *so* deplorable and unhealthy, that they still had some margin of choice. For the adult who has the final decision-making power, normally the father in the family, the purchase of the good can be the evidence that he has not lost his place as a social citizen, he still is a consumer in the marketplace and a provider of satisfactions to his family. For the adolescent who enjoys them, the artifacts allow a public presentation of him/herself and of his/her social condition as relatively privileged, or not so unfortunate. The most pragmatic side of this type of consumer behavior was expressed by mothers, who see the electrical appliances as an investment, following two lines of reasoning: first, if money is not invested in consumer durables when some is available, it disappears with no trace in nondurable expenses; second, the objects are securities to be sold or pawned for cash when need arrives.

In macro-social terms, the presence of these appliances and of well-dressed adolescents cannot be derived from a theory that sets out "basic human needs" and studies the historical and cultural ways in which these needs are satisfied. The character of human needs cannot be comprehended without explicit reference to the actual means and ways in which they are satisfied in particular social systems (Leiss, 1976, p. 8). These objects are prototypes of the logic of a consumer society, in which individuals orient their needs toward the type of satisfactions embodied in a growing number and variety of goods.

The Challenge of and to Democracy

The elections in 1983 and the inauguration of a democratically elected government in December of that year implied a major change in Argentina. Hopes were high; so were repressed social demands. This is not the place to analyze the social, economic and political aspects of the transition to democracy (Jelin, ed., 1985a and 1985b; CEPAL, 1986; and various articles in DEBATES, 1984 and 1985). Also, it is a short time—at the time of this writing only two and a half years have elapsed—to be able to make a thorough evaluation or a balance of accomplishments in the reconstruction of a devastated society. I will only mention some of the new developments and trends that affect the urban fabric and the conditions of the poor.

Political democracy implied the open discussion and public visibility of the issue of poverty. One of the first important governmental reports was *La pobreza en la Argentina* (INDEC, 1984), reporting the extent of poverty in the country. The data are powerful: in the country as a whole about 22% lived under the poverty line; about 7% in the central city of Buenos Aires and 27% in the area of Greater Buenos Aires. These figures have undoubtedly grown during the 1980s, given the deepening of the economic crisis. But beyond the quantitative evidence what is relevant here is the fact that for the first time in the history of the country, there is an official and public recognition of the reality of poverty as a significant social phenomenon.

From recognition to action, however, the passage is not automatic. In a country in which cultural traditions are focused on individual and family social mobility on the one hand, and on the presence of a welfare state that is the Big Provider of services on the other, the economic and fiscal crisis has a very special impact. What appears at first sight is personal despair and complaints as to what the government is not doing. If we add the fact that whatever solidarity associations in existence at the local level were repressed and destroyed during the dictatorship, the challenge of democratization of the society is large and difficult to meet. No alternative ways, no mediating structures, can be called into action immediately.

The challenge, from this perspective, is large. The reconstruction of the social fabric of everyday life at a supra-family level, the generalization of participatory practices, the spread of local solidarity: these seem to be the ways— still to be created—for democratization of everyday life. How are these to be combined with the challenge to improve the living conditions of the poor and the need to strengthen and further legitimate representative political institutions? The answer, of course, is to be found in the future developments in the country.

Note

1. This study has led to a series of papers and publications devoted to specific theoretical, methodological and empirical issues. These include Jelin and Feijoo, 1980; Ramos, 1981 and 1982; Feijoo, 1983; Llovet, 1984; Jelin, 1984a, 1984b and 1984c; Jelin, Llovet and Ramos, 1982.

References

Beccaria, Luis, and Alvaro Orsatti, "Argentina 1970-1985: La dinámica del empleo en un período de inestabilidad económica y social." *Economía de América Latina*, No. 13. 1985.

Canitrot, Adolfo, "Teoría y práctica del liberalismo, política antiinflacionaria y apertura económica en la Argentina, 1976-1981." *Estudios CEDES*, Vol. 3, No. 10. 1981.

CEPAL, *Tres ensayos sobre inflación y política de estabilización.* Buenos Aires, CEPAL, Documento de trabajo 18. 1986.

Debates, 1984-1985, Nos. 1-4. Buenos Aires.

Feijoo, Maria del Carmen, *Buscando un techo: familia y vivienda popular.* Buenos Aires, Estudios CEDES. 1984.

INDEC, *La pobreza en la Argentina.* Buenos Aires, INDEC. 1984.

Jelin, Elizabeth, "Daily Lives of Urban Women," in *Women on the Move.* Paris, UNESCO. 1984a.

—*Familia y unidad doméstica. Mundo público y vida privada.* Buenos Aires, Estudios CEDES. 1984b.

—"Las relaciones sociales del consumo: el caso de las unidades domésticas de sectores populares," in CEPAL, *La mujer en el sector popular urbano.* Santiago, CEPAL. 1984c.

Jelin, Elizabeth (ed.), *Los nuevos movimientos sociales/1: Mujeres. Rock nacional.* Buenos Aires, CEAL. 1985a.

—*Los nuevos movimientos sociales/2: Derechos humanos. Obreros. Barrios.* Buenos Aires, CEAL. 1985b.

Jelin, Elizabeth, and María del Carmen Feijoo, *Trabajo y familia en el ciclo de vida femenina: el caso de los sectores populares de Buenos Aires.* Buenos Aires, Estudios CEDES. 1980.

Jelin, Elizabeth, Juan José Llovet and Silvina Ramos, "Un estilo de trabajo: La investigación microsocial." Buenos Aires, CEDES, *mimeo.* 1982.

Leiss, William, *The Limits of Satisfaction: An Essay on the Problem of Needs and Commodities.* Toronto, University of Toronto Press. 1976.

Llovet, Juan José, *Servicios de salud y sectores populares. Los años del proceso.* Buenos Aires, CEDES. 1984.

Oszlak, Oscar, "El derecho al espacio urbano." Buenos Aires, CEDES, *mimeo.* 1983.

Ramos, Silvina, *Maternidad en Buenos Aires: la experiencia popular.* Buenos Aires, CEDES. 1983.

—*Las relaciones de parentesco y de ayuda mutua en los sectores populares urbanos. Un estudio de caso.* Buenos Aires, CEDES. 1981.

Tedesco, Juan Carlos, Cecilia Braslavsky and Ricardo Carciofi, *El proyecto educativo autoritario: Argentina 1976-1982.* Buenos Aires, FLACSO. 1983.

6 Public Health Problems in Medellín, Colombia

By Héctor Abad Gómez

I
Poliatrics

My approach to public health is not the classical one as a fight against diseases. For me it is a discipline that regards human beings as capable of organizing their own societies to arrive finally at "complete physical, social and mental well-being" for everybody, which is the World Health Organization's definition for "health."

I have coined a word for a possible new discipline: "poliatrics," from the Greek roots: *polis* meaning city state, and *iatrics* meaning study, prevention, treatment. Poliatrics means "the treatment of the diseases of the city or state." The first health discipline was medicine: to cure diseases of the body and of the mind. Then came public health: to prevent and cure all kinds of diseases of human beings. Then social security: to avoid, prevent and provide for the sequela of all risks that a person is subject to from his conception to his death. Now it is time for poliatrics: to provide for the well-being of all society.[1]

I have defined poliatrics as a new scientific discipline which studies and applies the laws of well-being *of, for* and *in* human groups, studying historically specific cases, past and present, in which political, economic, social and cultural conditions have determined the presence or absence of well-being for local, national, continental or world human populations.

Science has until now occupied itself with natural phenomena, which may or may not have any relation to humans, and with biological, social and psychological phenomena which have an intimate relation to humanity, such as sickness, death and suffering. Medicine arose from the compassion that a human being felt before the suffering of another human, and with the decision to do something to alleviate that suffering. From medicine, there emerged public health, which is nothing more than the application of science to prevent and cure diseases and to rehabilitate those persons who have suffered their consequences, in an organized, disciplined, planned and coordinated way, within a human community.

This must go on. Medical attention and health are innate rights, acquired from the simple act of being born, due to all and every one of the human beings who are born in the world. To promote health, avoid suffering, cure diseases, care for the sick, rehabilitate the disabled, prevent endemic diseases and epidemics, console the sad, avoid premature aging, and care for children and the aged, are and will be tasks that medicine and public health cannot renounce.

But it is also time that doctors and health workers reflect on whether, because we have dedicated ourselves exclusively to the prevention and treatment of diseases and their consequences, we may have forgotten to observe the totality of human life in human communities, and its problems such as poverty, unemployment, injustice, violence, insecurity and deficiencies of social organization. What I am proposing, with the creation of a new discipline that can become a new profession, *poliatrics*, is that we emerge from our womb. Some of us, along with statesmen, sociologists, anthropologists, jurists, historians, communications experts, social scientists, religious leaders and people in general, must think, study, and establish relationships and practices around the development of a model of a new human society, in which it will not only be the absence of illness that preoccupies us, but the health of the *polis*. We should understand this as the ancient Greeks did, as a totality, a whole, and with a holistic vision of its welfare.

Problems like the overcrowding and overpopulation of certain areas, like interracial or international hatred, political and religious conflicts, wars and violence; obvious generators of ill-being, of human suffering, will be the problems that the poliatrists, the professionals of this new science, ought to study.

II
Medellín—The Background

It is within this context that I am going to speak about the health problems of my city of Medellín, Colombia. I will describe what my city is, and afterward, what the main "diseases" are.

Medellín is the second largest city in Colombia, with over 1.5 million of the country's 28 million inhabitants. Medellín is a major industrial center whose rise was based on an earlier growth of farming in the Department of Antioquia. The Spanish provincial governor, Mon y Velarde, instituted a land reform in 1783, which divided up some of the largest estates to increase production and taxes. Up to then, five families had owned most of the land, and gold had been the major product. The reform, which gave families land if they could begin commercial production in four years, stimulated development. I would trace the region's noted entrepreneurial spirit to these origins. In the mid-nineteenth century, a coffee boom created export opportunities and rural demand for industrial products. Medellín began to industrialize and became the center of the textile industry of Colombia. It is the headquarters of the three large Colombian firms in that industry.

In the last ten years, economic growth in manufacturing has not been as strong. The unemployment rate, which used to be lower than in other Colombian cities, has risen to 17% vs. 12.2% in Bogotá. This is in part due to foreign competition, which has been aggravated by government policy: the last two presidents have taken a free trade line and cut tariffs. In this situation, some of Medellín's entrepreneurs have moved to illegal exports to the U.S. cocaine market.

The city's income is unevenly distributed. The socio-economic distribution of the population of the city proper, in round figures, is shown in Table 1. From these figures we can say, in general, that only a little less than a third of the population live well. I want to point out that the table shows that around 60,000 people have *very low* incomes, while around 20,000 people have *high* incomes.

Table 1

Socio-Economic Distribution
of the Population of the City of Medellín, Colombia
(Round Figures)

Classification	Income per Year In U.S. $	Population	Percentage
High	More than 20,000	20,000	2%
Medium High	Between 10,000-20,000	175,000	11%
Medium-Medium	Between 6,000-10,000	200,000	13%
Medium Low	Between 3,000-6,000	575,000	37%
Low	Between 1,000-3,000	500,000	33%
Very Low	Less than 1,000	60,000	4%
Total		1,550,000	100%

Source: Anuario Estadístico, 1983

Comparisons of standards of living at four social levels, taken from a university survey, show wide disparities in housing (for the high income families there were 42 square meters per inhabitant, vs. 4 square meters for the very low income), unemployment, literacy and disease. See Tables 2 and 4.

Table 2

Socio-Economic Distribution of Living Quarters,
Education and Unemployment,
Medellín,
by Classification of Families

	High	Medium	Low	Very Low
Living Space				
Sq. Meters/Family	328	172	109	30
Sq. Meters/Inhabitant	42	31	13	4
Residents per bed	0.8	1.2	1.5	2.5
Education				
Illiteracy (%)	0	0	5	31
Attended University (%)	57.1	21.4	8	0
Unemployment				
Adult rate (%)	5.0	7.1	13.0	20.0

Source: Sample survey by students of Public Health, Faculty of
Medicine, University of Antioquia, 198. Definitions of Classification: See Table 1.

III
Health in Medellín

Health conditions in Medellín can be examined first by looking at the main causes of death in Medellín. (See Table 3) What is striking about this table is that heart disease and homicide were the most common causes of death. For most diseases the death-rate pattern looks more typical of a developed than an underdeveloped country. When I was young, deaths from typhoid and diptheria were common. But by focusing on public health, rather than just curing individual cases, these problems have been proven tractable.

Table 3

The Ten Main Causes of Death in Medellín, Colombia, 1983

Causes of death	Number of deaths	Rate 100,000 inhabitants	Main age group affected	More affected sex
1. Isquemic heart diseases	1,214	77	65+	Men
2. Homicides and battery	924	58	15-44	Men
3. Brain Vascular diseases	742	47	65+	Women
4. Lung and other heart circulatory diseases	618	39	65+	Women
5. Other diseases of the respiratory tract	497	31	65+	Women
6. Transit Accidents	470	30	15-44	Men
7. Malignant Tumors—No specified site	400	25	65+	Women
8. Perinatal period affections	391	25	1 month	Men
9. Intestinal malignant tumors	309	19	65+	Women
10. Respiratory malignant tumors	290	18	45-64	Men

Source: See Table 2.

The Department of Preventive Medicine and Public Health of the School of Medicine of the University of Antioquia, in Medellín, has developed a new technology of public health, beginning in the rural areas of this state (starting in 1958 in the municipality of Santo Domingo). This approach consists of the training, during three months at the local hospital, of young peasant women with primary education. They are trained in such elementary matters of health as transmission of intestinal parasitosis, importance of excreta disposals, pure water supplies and elementary personal hygiene, and also in elementary health techniques such as measuring blood pressure, first aid, weight and height of babies, signals of trouble in pregnancy, vaccinations, injections of medical prescriptions and even attendance of normal deliveries. These trained women are called "Rural Health Promoters" and are sent back to their own rural residences to apply this new knowledge, supervised by a nurse and a general practitioner working at the local hospital of the urban center of each municipality. Their work in three years of practice in 30 small rural communities has proven so successful that the infant mortality dropped in half; the percentage of all kinds of vaccinations was raised to 90 percent of the infant population; the index of housing with proper sewage disposal rose to 80 percent; and intestinal parasitosis declined.

The satisfaction of the rural population with the work of this new health personnel was such that a project of providing this new health worker to the whole country was undertaken by the recently founded School of the Public Health in Medellín, headed by the same Director of the Department of Preventive Medicine. The program was extended to rural areas of 14 states of Colombia in 1964. At this moment (1985), there are more than 4,000 Rural Health Promoters in the rural areas of our country.

This experience was brought to the city of Medellín, at the urban level, in 1973. In poor neighborhoods women volunteers were and are being trained as "Health Volunteers," who have similar duties to those described above. They have been able to reduce the infant mortality due to diarrheal diseases to virtually no deaths in recent years, by their action of early oral rehydration. Mothers have been trained to watch for symptoms, and the volunteers have supplies of electrolyte solutions in the *barrios*, for the children who need them. These are two examples of autochthonous health techniques that have sprouted from the felt needs of underdeveloped communities in a Latin American country. This approach was at first received with skepticism. The Manufacturers Association of Medellín at first was critical of the need for a Chair of Public Health which looked at economic patterns. But they began to support the new concept when it was shown that deaths could be prevented by focusing at the community level. The reduction of diseases of underdevelopment is not as advanced in all of Colombia as in Medellín. In many areas, the death-rate pattern looks more typical of an underdeveloped nation. Even within Medellín, there remain differences by social classification. Socio-economic conditions are basic in relation to health problems, as is well known. In a study that we made at the Department of Preventive Medicine and Public Health of the School of Medicine of the University of Antioquia, Medellín, Colombia, we found the striking differences shown in Table 4.

Table 4

Socio-Economic Distribution of Medical Conditions, Medellín, by Classification of Families

Condition (% rates)	High	Medium	Low	Very Low
Acute Respiratory Diseases	22	8	21	74
Gastro Enteritis	14	11	9	51
Whooping Cough	0	0	10	24
Poliomyelitis	0	0	0	1
Acute Hepatitis	6	8	11	7
Acute Dermatosis	10	0	10	28
Accidents	19	2	16	21
Handicaps	0	0	2	4
Acidopeptic Diseases	24	14	7	14
Mental Diseases	22	3	4	16
Tumors	3	3	2	1
Allergies	21	10	15	4
Surgery	32	10	15	4

Source: Medical histories taken in sample survey by students.
(See Table 2)

The students found that rates of gastroenteritis and active respiratory disease were more than three times as high for the lowest income groups than for the three higher groups. Ulcers, on the other hand, were most concentrated at the top and the bottom of the income ladder. These continuing disparities suggest again that public health must be conducted with a view to broader social problems.

IV
Violence as an Epidemic

One threat to the public health and well-being clearly requires a poliatric approach. In Table 3 above, the most striking figure is the second cause of death, that is, *homicides.* This cause takes its victims between the ages of 15 and 44. Almost all other causes of death are primarily found for ages sixty-five and more. Violence is the main cause of death in Colombia for men between 15 and 44 years of age.

In 1962, during the First Colombian Congress of Public Health, it was agreed that: "Violence constitutes one of the grave problems of Public Health in Colombia, not only by the number of deaths that it produces, but by their atrocious characteristics, the immense difficulty for its control, the few serious studies that have been made about the etiology and the social, economic and sociological impact that it produces upon the Colombian population."[2]

During an Ibero-Latinamerican Forum on "Health in the XXI Century," held in Medellín in July, 1984, this writer presented a paper on "Epidemiology of Violence," which arrived at the following conclusions:[3]

1. *Violence is not a genetic human phenomenon: violence is a cultural phenomenon, created by men under certain circumstances.*

If we consider that the history of humanity begins 2600 millenia back, it is only in the last eight or ten thousand years, since the agricultural revolution and the rise of patriarchal society, that the phenomenon of normal violence has been found among human communities.[4] Violence is cultural, and therefore our own artificial creation. This is put in evidence by the analysis of death rates from homicide in different countries and different eras.

2. *Human beings are pacific or violent, according to the circumstances in which they find themselves.*

In Colombia, where we traditionally have been violent, we had a homicide death rate in 1943 of 8.1 per 100,000 inhabitants, much lower than that today, and lower than that in the eight other countries (plus Puerto Rico) that have the greatest rates of homicide today. A few years later, the rate in Colombia became much higher because of a national political and economic crisis. We humans everywhere are essentially emotional and changeable, and therefore potentially violent but also potentially rational. Only in certain circumstances do we comport ourselves violently. I have asserted, and continue to believe, that fanaticism is the cause of violence. What we have to study more deeply is what produces fanaticism. The explanation is undoubtedly found in the education given us in childhood and youth. It is in the cultural, religious, national, racial and political ethnocentrism, which causes many human groups to become fanatic, and therefore, violent. Only when there is humanistic general education, when we all feel and think that we belong to one species, essentially emotional but fortunately potentially rational, will we be able to exercise, and to regulate ourselves by, our reason. Manicheanism, the theory that claims that only we are the good and that the others are bad, is at root, at the origin, of all violence.

3. Violence is not always a disease in itself, but a symptom of profound social disease.

Violence is not always unjustified, pathological, and irrational. There are conditions of oppression, of injustice, of enormous economic inequalities, in which violence is not a disease, but rather a necessity of the social organism. It is a little like the response of a biological organism to infection. It would be, in this case, like fever, which is one of the mechanisms by which the body combats the infection that is the true disease. In the first work on violence that my students of Preventive Medicine and Public Health carried out under my coordination in 1983, they found: "the genesis of violence is explained on the basis of needs for essential necessities and for control of one's own territory; on seeing these endangered, people rebel. Then relations of domination will be felt in the oppressed as violence, and in the oppressor as justice and order."[5]

It is not the human being in the abstract that is violent, but rather the human being placed in specific circumstances. It is the circumstances that turn him violent that must be studied in depth, to avoid them or correct them, and thus eliminate violent destruction among human beings.

4. Great national, religious, ethnic, economic, educational, political or, in summary, cultural differences are the generators of violence.

I believe that a brief analysis of the current world situation gives us a basis to consider this fourth conclusion valid:

Why do they fight in Ireland?
Because some are Catholics and some are Protestants.

Why do they fight in Lebanon?
Because some are Christians and some are Moslems.

Why do they fight in the United States?
Because some are Black and some are white.

Why do they fight in Israel?
Because some are Jews and some are Arabs.

Why do they fight in Central America?
Because some are very rich and some are very poor.

Why do Iran and Iraq fight?
Because some are Shi'ites and some are Sunnis.

Why do we fight in Colombia?
For many reasons. Because some drug traffickers want the money and power that others have; or because they have lost out in other businesses; or because they have contracted *sicarios,* poor beings who kill for money, to settle accounts among themselves by force of arms.

Because the situation is intolerable for unemployed youth in poor neighborhoods; because they rob and kill for a few pesos and are later killed by death squads.

Because families are very poor and their members kill each other when they get drunk and fight. Or because being too rich they fight over inheritances. Or because they have to affirm themselves as masculine when they are insulted or depreciated. Or for jealousies and political hatreds. Or because they have to eliminate those who seek land on the properties of latifundistas. Or because one must do away with the thieves, the robbers, the subversives, the communists, the Blacks, the beggars, so they will not bother the powerful classes. Or because they have to kill the police who defend the system. Or because they have to kidnap to sustain the guerrillas.

They all kill with good intentions, believing themselves to be the best, the saviors of good customs, of the nation and its institutions, of the church, or of the revolution. And all of this is incited by the opposed doctrines of national security or world revolution. And thus our mortality rates from violence climb sky-high.

Let me quote an interesting article which appeared in the magazine *Science,* of the American Association for the Advancement of Science, in December, 1984:

One American kills another every 23 minutes. Homicide has doubled in this country in the past 20 years and is now claiming more than 20,000 lives a year. Many of our law enforcement agents have given up trying to figure out why. According to a recent FBI report, "Murder is primarily a societal problem over which law enforcement has little or no control." Public health officials say it's time they had a crack at reducing the devastation.

"Violence is every bit a public health issue for me and my successors in this century as smallpox, tuberculosis, and syphilis were for my predecessors in the last two centuries," says U.S. Surgeon General C. Everett Koop. "Violence in American public and private life has indeed assumed the proportions of an epidemic."

An epidemic is defined as a condition occurring at a rate exceeding its natural occurrence. American homicide qualifies because it has increased so dramatically since the 1960s. At least 80 percent of the countries that report homicide statistics to the United Nations have rates lower than the U.S. rate of almost 10 for every 100,000 citizens...

One manifestation of the recent public health interest in homicide is the formation of the Violence Epidemiology Branch at the federal Centers for Disease Control in Atlanta.

"One of the main missions of the CDC is to prevent premature and unnecessary death," says Mark Rosenberg, chief of the newly formed unit. "Contrary to the hopelessness that currently exists among the public, a significant number of homicides can be prevented."

This optimism derives, in part, from past triumphs over many of the world's most pernicious afflictions and a belief that the comprehensive approach of the public health discipline will lead to solutions that previous, more circumscribed efforts have not.[6]

Now, let us see what the present picture of the world as a whole is, in relation to violence, to compare it with the situation in Colombia and in Medellín. National figures are given in Tables 5 and 6.

Table 5

Countries with Greatest Rates of Homicide
(Last Available Figures)

	Country	Rate 100,000 People	Year
1.	Guatemala	157	1976
2.	El Salvador	113	1980
3.	Colombia	57	1980
4.	Mexico	49	1978
5.	Chile	38	1979
6.	Egypt	27	1978
7.	Argentina	20	1977
8.	Federal Germany	20	1980
9.	Puerto Rico	13	1977
10.	U.S.A.	11	1979

Source: U.N. Demographic Yearbook

Table 6

**Countries with Lowest Rates of Homicide
(Last Available Figures)**

	Country	Rate 100,000 People	Year
1.	Greece	1	1978
2.	Spain	1	1978
3.	Belgium	2	1978
4.	Hungary	2	1978
5.	Portugal	2	1975
6.	Switzerland	2	1979
7.	Italy	3	1976
8.	Czechoslovakia	3	1978
9.	Japan	3	1979
10.	Austria	4	1979

Source: U.N. Demographic Yearbook

Metropolitan Medellín has a population of 2.2 million people living in a rather narrow valley that we call "Aburra Valley," in which there are, besides the city of Medellín, three other urban concentrations, each one of more than one hundred thousand people. In 1983 there were 1,112 homicides, which is a rate of 55 per 100,000 population, and in 1984 1,475 homicides, which is 32.5% more than in the previous year and a rate of 67 per 100,000 inhabitants, and which is, as we have seen, a very high rate.

Public health problems are changing in my city and in the world. Hunger, famine, poverty, all results of inequality and injustice, are still rampant. Violence is only a symptom, like fever, that the social organism is reacting against those more profound social diseases, ignorance and fanaticism of all kinds.

Drug dependency, narcotraffic, social injustice and mental diseases are all the results of a badly organized world society in which the distribution of wealth, education and justice is so different from the statistically normal distribution.

Are we going to have a better world in order to have better cities? That is our challenge. We have many things to do within our cities, but even more outside our cities. In Latin America, for example, if we do not achieve land reform and decentralized industrialization, we are going to continue to have hunger, poverty, unemployment and bad housing—and as a result of all this, violence. We are overcrowded. But overcrowding is just a symptom of other more profound social diseases, especially economic diseases. As I see the cities of the United States of America I see them more and more Latin-Americanized. As I see the big cities of Latin America, I see them more and more Asiatized. I have been in Asia, in Manila, Djakarta and New Delhi. And I agree with the American writer who, after a trip to Asia, said: "I have seen the future, and I do not like it." If we want to build a better future we have a lot to do within and outside our monstrous megalopolis.

Notes

1. The rest of this section is based on Héctor Abad Gómez, "La poliatría y la teoría Meso-Panómica," paper delivered to the VIII Colombian Congress of Public Health, Medellín, July 1984. See also, *Curso de poliatría: documentos básicos: el proceso de los problemas colombianos,* Universidad de Antioquia: Facultad de Medicina, Dept. de Medicina Preventiva y Salud Pública, 1973.

2. Héctor Abad Gómez, "Necesidad de estudios epidemiológicos sobre la violencia" *Primer Congreso Colombiano de Salud Publica,* page. 253, Editorial Bedout, Medellín 1962.

3. Héctor Abad Gómez, "Epidemiology of violence" presented at a forum, "Health for the XXI Century," Medellín 1984. The following four points are condensed from this paper.

4. Evelyn Reed, "Feminismo y naturaleza humana," *Revista Viejo Topo* 33 (Nov. 1979), pp. 37-38.

5. Student report, Faculty of Medicine, course in Public Health and Preventive Medicine, 1983.

6. Nikki Meredith, "The Murder Epidemic," *Science,* December, 1984, Volume 5, No. 10. pp. 43-48.

7 Housing Policy in Mexico City

by Kathryn Stephens-Rioja

Housing is an issue that appears frequently in Mexico City newspapers. The National Plan of Development elaborated in 1984 by the Miguel de la Madrid administration identifies housing as a primary concern for the country. Government efforts to initiate programs to accommodate housing needs in Mexico City have varied according to the country's political and economic climate. The most significant advance in housing policy for the city occurred in the early 1970s following the 1968 period of social unrest. Currently Mexican housing policy makers are facing the issue of how to provide assistance to the increasing number of residents of this rapidly growing metropolitan area. The dramatic rise in construction costs experienced in the 1980s as a result of high inflation rates and a fluctuating currency value have indeed made this a complex issue. The objective of this paper is to explore this issue in the light of three basic questions: What are the housing needs in Mexico City? What programs has the government developed to meet these needs? What are the current trends in housing policy for the metropolitan area?

Housing Needs in Mexico City

It is helpful to consider housing needs in the context of the city's growth. During the past three decades, Mexico City has experienced very dynamic growth. With a total population of 16.9 million according to the 1980 census, the Metropolitan Area of Mexico City (MAMC) is now one of the largest in the world. The estimated population for the year 2000 is close to 30 million.[1]

The MAMC includes 16 *delegaciones* of the Federal District, which is the seat of the federal government, and 13 municipalities of the adjacent State of Mexico.[2] Population growth in the MAMC occurred entirely within Federal District boundaries until 1950. From 1950 to 1960, growth extended into three muncipalities of the State of Mexico, and from 1960 to 1970, into ten more.[3] One area on the Eastern border of the Federal District, Nezahualcoyotl, increased in population from 62,000 to 670,000 from 1964 to 1970.[4] Most growth is now occurring in the State of Mexico in the north and northeastern parts of the metropolitan area, although there is still some growth in the southeastern section of the Federal District.

The rapid rate of population growth is no doubt a significant factor affecting housing needs in the MAMC. There is tremendous demand for housing; the housing deficit in the MAMC in 1970 was estimated to be 577,000 units, equal to 44.6% of the existing stock (including units needed for new household formation, for rehabilitation and to relieve overcrowding).[5] According to the National

Housing Plan of 1984, there is some indication of an increase in the problem of overcrowding. The number of people per household in the country as a whole was 4.9 in 1950, 5.5 in 1969, 5.8 in 1970, and 6.2 in 1980. According to the same Plan, 40% of the households in 1980 had one room.[6]

The most significant housing issue in the MAMC is affordability. It has been estimated that approximately 55% of the MAMC population cannot afford housing produced by the private sector.[7] In the 1980s, housing prices and rental rates have soared due to increasing inflation and the fluctuating value of the peso. According to one study, during the 1974-1980 period the price index and minimum wage increased at approximately the same rate while the price of low income housing rose at a rate 32% higher.[8] In 1983, the price index increased at a rate 48% higher than the minimum wage, and the price of low income housing, at a rate 69% higher. Condominium prices, according to the same study, rose 94% in 1983 and rental rates, 500% in the 1980-1984 period.[9]

For many MAMC residents, the solution to the affordability problem has been self-built housing. From 1970 to 1974, close to 60% of the housing produced in the country was self-built.[10] As this process normally operates, a family will secure a plot of land, build a simple structure using either cement blocks or recycled materials, and as time and resources permit, construct additional rooms or stories. Much of the current growth in the MAMC is happening through the self-built housing process.

The factor that enables this process to occur is the existence of a substantial informal land market through which plots of land can be obtained at affordable prices. In the informal market, land is sub-divided and sold without the title deeds, and housing is constructed without official permits.

One of the reasons the informal land market exists is the unique nature of Mexico's land tenure system. In Mexico, in addition to private and government-owned land, there is a form of collective property that was formally incorporated into the country's Constitution during the post-revolutionary period of the 1920s. Called *ejidal* or *comunal* according to how tenureship is established, this land is to be used for agricultural production, and may not be sold, mortgaged or otherwise enter the private land market.

Much of the settled land in the MAMC was originally collective property. In 1940, 75.5% of the land surrounding the Federal District was *ejidal* or *comunal*, and during the period of 1940-70, 50% of the growth of the MAMC was on collective property.[11] In 1980, collective property represented 60% and 70% of the unurbanized lands in the Federal District and the State of Mexico, respectively.[12]

A majority of the land sold in the informal land market is collective property that is no longer being used for agricultural purposes. Because the market value of the land is higher than the income generated through agricultural production, the *ejidal* and *comunal* owners are motivated to sell the land. Since there are no title deeds for the transaction, lots are often resold to various owners, causing property conflicts. In the 1970s, the government initiated a program to mitigate such conflicts by legalizing land tenure and granting title deeds in these areas.

The provision of basic services is a problem in these areas. Because they are zoned for agricultural use, the lands have not yet been subdivided and urban infrastructure, such as roadways, public transportation, water systems and electricity, has not been installed. In 1970, 41.2% of the population of the State of Mexico had no sewage provision, 21.8%, no electricity, and 28.8%, no potable water. The percentages for the Federal District were relatively lower at 11.6%, 2.6%, and 5.7% respectively.[13] The government has made an effort to provide infrastructure in informal land market areas such as in the case of the Nezahuacoyotl community settled in the 1960s. Growth, however, is occurring at such a rapid rate, particularly in the State of Mexico, that it is difficult for the government to provide these areas with the necessary services. The lack of public transportation is problematic as many of the residents of these neighborhoods live long distances from the workplace.

These factors, the tenureship situation and infrastructure conditions, make land sold in the informal land market inexpensive and thus accessible to a majority of the population. Self-built housing is the de facto housing solution for a significant percentage of the Mexico City residents. There is some indication that the cost of self-built housing is increasing substantially due to the rise in the price of building materials that has occurred in the 1980s as a result of peso value fluctuations and high inflation rates. According to one study, for example, the cost of a one room cement block structure increased from 9,000 pesos (US $375) in 1978 to 100,000 pesos (US $500) in 1984.[14] Even so, however, the self-built housing process on land purchased in the informal land market continues to be the way many families provide for their housing needs in the MAMC.

In addition to the informal land market activities, there are additional housing solutions, particularly for recent migrants who many times need immediate affordable shelter. These include living with family, relatives or friends, renting lands where a housing structure may be constructed, and building households in roof top areas.

Housing Programs in the Metropolitan Area

To discuss housing programs in the MAMC it is helpful to consider the context of Mexico's national housing policy. This is because the national housing agencies have concentrated a significant amount of funds in the MAMC. Much of the public housing constructed in the MAMC has, in fact, been financed through national agencies, although programs have also been developed in the area by local housing agencies. A consideration of national as well as local housing policy will, therefore, be useful to our discussion.

Housing policy tends to reflect the political and economic climate of the country. There are times when the government has done very little to meet housing needs, and times when it has made a serious effort to develop housing programs. Housing policy is part of the social reform program proposed by the leading party, the Partido Revolucionario Institucional (PRI) to mitigate social tensions. (Since it was founded in 1929, the PRI has won every presidential and governorship campaign, and has maintained a majority position in the Senate and House of Representatives.) Housing programs are often initiated following periods of social unrest to make the system flexible to change such as occurred in the 1970s during the Echeverría administration. The housing programs developed at that time form part of the social reform program initiated by Echeverría in response to the 1968 period of political unrest.

Federal Housing Programs in MAMC

There are three main periods in the federal housing programs: 1925-1963, during which housing policy concentrated on the construction by public agencies of large scale multiunit housing projects for sale at subsidized prices; 1963-1972, when there was a shift in housing policy toward finance instead of direct production by public agencies; and 1972 to the present, when the National Housing Fund, a benefit program that placed some responsibility for housing finance on the private sector by requiring employers to contribute to a fund for employee housing, was begun, as well as programs to provide technical and financial assistance in support of the self-help housing process. Also of significance are the rental housing program initiated during the first period, and the land legalization program begun during the third period. Following, we shall briefly describe the various programs created during each of these periods.

The first public housing program in Mexico was established in 1925 by the Dirección General de Pensiones Civiles y Retiro (DGPCR), a social security agency. This agency, which in 1960 became the Instituto de Seguridad Social para Trabajadores al Servicio del Estado (ISSSTE), currently one of the principal health and social security agencies, built low cost housing for government workers. The program was very modest; annual production from 1925-1946 was 308 households, and from 1946-1960, 1,570.[15] In 45 years, the total number of units financed by this agency was 66,848. (See Table 1.)

In 1942 the Banco Nacional de Obras Públicas (BANOBRAS) began a housing program. BANOBRAS built large multiunit housing projects that were then sold at subsidized prices to qualifying low income families. This also started as a relatively modest program with an annual production of 1370 units.[16] In 42 years, BANOBRAS financed or constructed a total of 108,064 households.

During this period a Rent Freeze Program and a Rental Housing Program were also begun. The Rent Freeze Program was established in the 1930s by the president at that time, Lázaro Cárdenas, and is still effective today for the housing units in the central core of the city that were declared to be part of the rent freeze district. The last rent freeze decree was issued in 1948. There is a Rent Control Proposal currently in review by the Federal Legislature. As it is a most controversial issue, it will likely remain in Congress for some time.

The Rental Housing Program was begun in 1953, and consisted of the construction of multiunit public housing projects that were rented at subsidized rates to

Table 1

Housing Activity by Agency

	Total Units	Number of Years in Operation
Federal Agencies		
INFONAVIT*	400,341	12
FOVI*	380,990	21
FOVISSSTE*	128,496	12
INDECO	111,973	11
BANOBRAS	108,064	42
FONHAPO*	80,176	3
DGPCR	66,848	45
Local Agencies		
DGHP	39,460	5
CODEUR	14,384	8
DDF	11,200	7
FIVIDESU*	5,000	1

*Currently sponsoring housing programs.
Source: SEDUE, *Programa nacional de desarrollo urbano y vivienda 1984-1988; SEDUE, Informe del programa de vivienda;* Garza, Gustavo and Schteingart, Martha, *La acción habitacional del Estado en México,* 1978.

low and middle income families. The government still operates the rental program of these buildings today, although in 1963 it discontinued the construction of new rental housing projects. The annual number of households produced while the program was in effect is 1,471.[17] 19 of the 39 currently existing rental housing projects are located in the MAMC.[18] Although the program has had some decapitalization problems, it has been successful in maintaining reasonable rental rates. The agencies responsible for program administration are the Instituto Mexicano de Seguridad Social (IMSS), and the ISSSTE.

The second period began in 1963 with the initiation of the Housing Finance Program, which is a program designed to increase the amount of financial resources available for low income housing. Through this program banks (all of which as of 1982 have been nationalized) are required to put 30% of the savings deposit resources into a pool for financing low income housing. This sum is discounted from the amount that banks are required by law to deposit in the National Bank of Mexico. The banks must show that these funds have been applied to loans for low income housing. The agency created to supervise this program is the Fondo de Operación y Descuento Bancario (FOVI). FOVI receives and reviews loan applications, and upon approval, directs applicants to the financial institution granting the loan. This program, still in operation, has been quite successful. The annual number of housing units financed has increased from 14,170 to 21,714 to 76,736 units.[19] The total number of units financed through the program in the 21 years since it was begun is 380,990.

Also founded during this period is the Instituto Nacional para el Desarrollo de la Comunidad y de la Vivienda (INDECO). INDECO was established in

1970 to finance the construction and rehabilitation of low income housing both in urban and rural areas. This was a relatively modest program; the annual production began at 4,398 units and increased to 17,117 units in 1976.[20] The program operated.until 1981 when it was decentralized to the state governments.

The third period, 1972 to the present, is the most significant time in the development of Mexican housing policy. During this period the National Housing Fund was begun. This program was developed as part of a social reform effort started as a result of the political crisis of the late 1960s. The National Housing Fund, created through a reform of article 123 of the Mexican Constitution, is a program that requires all employers to contribute a bonus equal to 5% of the total employee wages to a housing fund. From this fund low interest housing loans are provided to employees. There are two agencies responsible for administering these funds: the Instituto del Fondo Nacional de la Vivienda para los Trabajadores (INFONAVIT) grants loans to all non-government wage earners; and the Fondo de Vivienda para los Trabajadores del Estado (FOVISSSTE) provides this service for government employees. The INFONAVIT has a three-way structure with representatives from the labor, private and government sectors.

The National Housing Fund program is significant because it provides a way for employers to fulfill the employee housing obligation established in the Constitution of 1917, and because it creates an additional funding source for public interest housing. INFONAVIT has been the most active of all housing agencies in Mexico; the agency's yearly production has increased from 25,250 to 37,714 to 55,385 units for a total of 400,341 units in 12 years.[21] INFONAVIT originally financed and constructed housing. In 1974, however, the agency suspended the construction program due to pressures from private sector groups that felt the public sector was a competitor in the industry, and from labor organizations that wanted more control in the housing production process. INFONAVIT's programs consist basically of the construction of completed housing and therefore benefit mostly middle income wage earners.

INFONAVIT is still operating successfully today, although it has had some decapitalization problems due to the peso value fluctuations and rising inflation. The economic crisis of the early 1980s that resulted in the devaluation of the peso and the nationalization of banks in the country has affected the agency's operation. According to one study, in 1983, with five times more money, INFONAVIT built 28% fewer units than nine years earlier.[22] In 1983, with a total of 58 million pesos, this agency funded 46,738 units. In 1984, with 106 million pesos, the agency funded 47,033 units. Although it has decapitalization problems, INFONAVIT is still one of Mexico's most significant housing programs currently.

Also during this period programs relating to the self-help housing process were initiated. One is the Land Legalization Program. This program was begun in 1973 as a result of land-related conflicts that occurred in the MAMC. In the early 1970s, disputes regarding land tenureship and the provision of infrastructure arose in Nezahuacoyotl on the eastern boundary of the Federal District, an area which had been settled primarily through the operation of the informal land market. At that time, residents of Nezahuacoyotl organized a payment strike in an effort to obtain title deeds and basic services. As a result of pressure from both residents of this area and developers, the government became more actively involved in the municipality by funding infrastructure projects and initiating a program to grant title deeds to the land.

The agency created to administer this program is the Comisión para la Regularización de la Tenencia de la Tierra (CORETT). This federal agency operates a nationwide program for granting title deeds for *ejidal* and *comunal* lands sold through the informal land market. The legalization of private or state owned land is performed by local agencies.

Also relating to the self-help housing process and begun during this period is the Fideicomiso del Fondo de Habitaciones Populares (FONHAPO) founded in 1981. FONHAPO grants loans for low income housing projects to state and municipal institutions, and to community groups such as housing cooperatives. This agency is significant in that it funds projects supportive of the self-help housing process, such as land acquisition, installation of water and sanitary systems, and the construction of one-unit housing projects that later can be built up or enlarged. The agency's programs also include the financing of cooperatives to produce building materials for use in the housing projects.

FONHAPO was originally part of BANOBRAS, the Public Works Bank. It was decentralized in 1981 when it became a *fideicomiso*, or trust fund, and since then has become a very active housing agency. In the three years since its founding, this agency has financed a total of 80,176 housing projects.

A majority of the public housing built in the MAMC has been financed or produced through federal housing programs. In 1973, for example, the agencies administering the employee benefit program, INFONAVIT and FOVISSSTE, invested 40.5% and 58.7% of total resources in the Federal District, respectively.[24] From 1973 to 1980, there is some indication of an effort by these agencies to decentralize housing investment from the Federal District. In 1980, for example, the percentage of funds invested by INFONAVIT in the Federal District was 19.1, and by FOVISSSTE, 26.8.[25] Even with these decentralization efforts, however, federal agencies continue to play a significant role in the financing of housing programs in the MAMC.

Local Housing Programs in MAMC

Although much of the housing built in the MAMC has been financed or produced through federal programs, there are also local housing programs operating there. The Department of the Federal District (DDF), for example, has sponsored several housing programs. As early as the 1930s, the DDF began to develop housing programs, although it wasn't until 1964 that the Department built the first large housing complexes. These were the San Juan project with 9,927 housing units, and the Santa Cruz project with 3,000 housing units.[26] In

1971, the first Federal District public housing agency was founded. This agency, the Dirección General de Habitaciones Populares (DGHP), operated from 1971-1975, producing 12 multiunit projects during that time.[27] The total number of units built by the DGHP was 39,460.

In 1975, the DGHP was replaced with the Comisión de Desarrollo Urbano (CODEUR). CODEUR is a multi-purpose agency that administrates a variety of urban programs including transportation and economic development. CODEUR, for example, played a significant role in the street construction and widening project of the late 1970s, and in the building of a market and warehouse area in the south- eastern part of the city. In 1983 CODEUR discontinued the public housing program, although it is still active in urban development projects. The agency produced a total of 14,384 housing units during the eight years it operated a public housing program.

In 1984, the DDF created the Fideicomiso de Vivienda y Desarrollo Social y Urbano (FIVIDESU). FIVIDESU is currently in the process of developing programs for the Federal District, including a Self-help Housing program in which participants can donate labor hours instead of making a down payment. The cost of a housing unit acquired in this program is approximately 5,000 dollars (1 million pesos) to be paid in a period of 15-20 years at 12% interest rate. Monthly payments are about US $30.00 to US $40.00 (6,000 to 7,000 pesos). Since 1984, FIVIDESU has initiated 38 self-help projects in various parts of the Federal District. In these projects a total of 5,004 units have been built.[28] Although the program is still in the beginning stages, it has had good results.

There are also housing programs in the State of Mexico. The Departamento de Desarrollo Urbano del Estado de Mexico, administered by the state government, has been developing low income housing programs since the 1960s. This agency works with the Instituto de Acción Urbano (AURIS) which is a state operated urban development agency. AURIS is currently beginning a self-help housing project partially funded by FONHAPO. This project will consist of the construction of 6,500 dwelling units.[29]

Current Trends in Housing Policy

The principal issues affecting housing policy in Mexico today are the peso exchange value and the rate of inflation. The cost of housing construction has increased dramatically in the 1980s, making the housing funded by the public sector, in particular finished housing, more difficult for families to afford. Agencies are now trying to develop alternative programs such as sites and services and self-help housing in an effort to provide housing that will be affordable. These efforts are consistent with informal land market activity which for a majority of the people in the metropolitan area of Mexico City is the de facto housing solution. The Self-help Housing program often works, for example, in coordination with the Land Legalization Program.

The Programa Nacional de Desarrollo Urbano y Vivienda for 1984 to 1988 contains the current housing policy guidelines. According to this National

Housing Program, of the total number of loans given for public housing in 1984, 51.3% will be for completed housing; 33.6% for sites and services and self-help projects; 13.3% for housing rehabilitation, and 1.8% for additional programs. The figures for 1983 are, respectively, 55.9, 28.1, 1.6, and 10.9, indicating that in 1984, there will be some decrease in loans for completed housing, and at the same time, some increase in loans for sites and services, self-help and housing rehabilitation programs.[30]

By public agency, the guidelines for the distribution of housing credits, according to the National Plan, are: FOVI, 33.1%; INFONAVIT, 31.3%; FONHAPO, 24.1%; FOVISSSTE, 6.4%; and all other agencies, 5.1%. For 1983, the respective figures were 34.6%, 33.8%; 10.5%; 9.7%; and 11.4%.[31] There will probably continue to be an emphasis on housing funding rather than direct production by public agencies due to difficulties of program administration and pressures from private sector construction interests.

In the metropolitan area of Mexico City, housing policy will be similar to that established for the national context. There will probably continue to be a concentration of public housing funds in the MAMC, in particular in the Federal District, although there is some indication in recent years of a significant effort to decentralize housing funds to other states within the country. The State of Mexico is likely to experience a rapid increase in the demand for affordable housing as a result of the tremendous growth now occurring there. The informal land market will probably continue to be the housing solution for a majority of families in this area. Policy makers in the metropolitan area of Mexico City are now developing self-help, site and services and housing rehabilitation programs that complement the informal land market process.

Notes

1. Secretaría de Programación y Presupuesto (SPP), Coordinación General de Servicios Nacional de Estadística, Geografía e Informática, *Censo general de población y vivienda*, 1980 (México: 1981), p. 3.

2. *Delegaciones* are essentially the same as municipalities except that the chief administrator of each *delegación* is appointed by the Mexico City mayor while the chief administrator of each municipality is elected.

3. Gustavo Garza and MarTha Schteingart, "Mexico City: The Emerging Metropolis" in *Metropolitan Latin America: The Challenge and the Response*, Wayne Cornelius and Robert Kemper, eds. (Beverly Hills: Sage Publications, 1978), p. 69.

4. Martha Schteingart, "El proceso de formación y consolidación de un asentamiento popular en México: El caso de la Ciudad Nezahuacoyotl" in the *Revista Interamericana de Planificación*, Vol. XV, Num 57 (México: 1981). p. 103.

5. Peter Ward, "Mexico City," in *Problems and Planning in Third World Cities*, ed. Michael Pacione (New York: St. Martin's Press, 1981), p. 41.

6. SEDUE, *Programa nacional de desarrollo urbano y vivienda, 1984-1988*, p. 29.

7. Beatriz García Peralta Nieto, "La autoconstrucción de la vivienda en la Ciudad de México," in *Lecturas del CEESTEM*, Vol I, Num 3 (México: 1981), p. 11-15.

8. Martha Schteingart, "El sector inmobilario y la vivienda en la crisis" in *Comercio Exterior*, Vol 34, Num 8 (México: agosto de 1984), p. 742.

9. Schteingart, "El sector inmobilario y la vivienda en la crisis," p. 748.

10. Gustavo Garza and Martha Schteingart, *La acción habitacional del Estado en México* (México: El Colegio de México, 1978), p. 66.

11. Gustavo Garza and Martha Schteingart, "Mexico City: The Emerging Metropolis," p. 72.

12. Interview with Arq. Javier Caraveo, Director of the Planning Department of the Federal District, March, 1982.

13. Departamento de Desarrollo Urbano, Gobierno del Estado de México, *Programa estatal de vivienda*, (México: 1981).

14. Schteingart, "El sector inmobilario y la vivienda en la crísis," p. 749.

15. Garza and Schteingart, *La acción habitacional del Estado en México*, p. 80.

16. Garza and Schteingart, *La acción habitacional del Estado en México*, p. 80.

17. Garza and Schteingart, *La acción habitacional del Estado en México*, p. 80.

18. Garza and Schteingart, *La acción habitacional del Estado en México*, pp. 211 and 216.

19. Garza and Schteingart, *La acción habitacional del Estado en México*, p. 80 and SEDUE, Informe de la SEDUE, p. 69.

20. Garza and Schteingart, *La acción habitacional del Estado en México*, p. 80.

21. Garza and Schteingart, p. 80 and SEDUE, *Informe de la SEDUE*, p. 69.

22. Schteingart, "El sector inmobilario y la vivienda en la crisis," p. 745.

23. SEDUE, *Informe de la SEDUE*, p. 69.

24. Manuel Perlo Cohen and Beatriz García Peralto Nieto, "Políticas habitacionales del sexenio: un balance inicial," in *Revista Habitacional*, Año I, Núm 2 and 3, (México: abril- septiembre, 1981), p. 41.

25. Perlo Cohen and Garcia Peralta Nieto, p. 41.

26. Garza and Schteingart, *La acción habitacional del Estado en México*, p. 115.

27. Garza and Schteingart, *La acción habitacional del Estado en México*, p. 121.

28. Interview with Arq. Laura Arizabe, Director of Self-help Housing Program, FIVIDESU, Federal District, November, 1984.

29. Interview with Project Manager of AURIS housing project, FONHAPO, June, 1984.

30. SEDEU, *Programa nacional de desarrollo urbano y vivienda*, pp. 85-86.
31. SEDUE, *Programa nacional de desarrollo urbano y vivienda*, pp. 85-86.

References

Castells, Manuel. "Apuntes para un análisis de clase de la política urbana del estado mexicano." *Revista Mexicana de Sociología*, Vol. IV, México, 1977, pp. 1161-1191.

CORETT (Comisión para la Regularización de la Tenencia de la Tierra). *Síntesis sobre el programa*, México, 1981.

DDF (Departamento del Distrito Federal), Oficina General de Planificación. *Plan de desarrollo urbano del Distrito Federal*, México, 1980.

García Peralta Nieto, Beatriz. "La autoconstrucción de la vivienda en la Ciudad de México." *Lecturas del CEESTEM*, Vol I, Num 3, 1981, pp. 11-15.

Garza, Gustavo and Schteingart, Martha. *La acción habitacional del Estado en México*. México: El Colegio de México, 1978.

—"Mexico City: The Emerging Metropolis." *Metropolitan Latin America: The Challenge and the Response*. Beverly Hills: Sage Publications, 1978, pp. 51-86.

Perlo Cohen, Manuel. "Política y vivienda en México, 1910-1952." *Revista mexicana de sociología*, Año XLI, Vol XLI, Num 3, México, julio-septiembre, 1979.

—"Políticas urbanas del DDF, 1920-1980." *Revista Vivienda*, Vol 6, Num 6, noviembre-diciembre, 1981.

Perlo Cohen, Manuel and García Peralta Nieto, Beatriz. "Estado, sindicalismo oficial y politicas habitacionales: análisis de una decada del INFONAVIT." *El obrero mexicano: Condiciones de trabajo*. México: Siglo XXI, 1984, pp. 94-133.

—"Políticas habitacionales del sexenio: un balance inicial." *Revista Habitación*, Año I, Num 2 and 3, México, abril-septiembre, 1981.

Departamento de Desarrollo Urbano, Gobierno del Estado de México. *Programa estatal de vivienda*. México: 1981.

Schteingart, Martha. "El proceso de formación y consolidación de un asentamiento popular en México: El caso de la Ciudad Nezahuacoyotl." *Revista Interamericana de Planificación*, Vol XV, Num 57, pp. 110-114.

—"La acción habitacional del estado mexicano: un balance." *Habitación*, Vol 7/8, Num 2, México, julio-diciembre, 1982, pp. 89-101.

—"El sector inmobiliario y la vivienda en la Crísis" *Comercio Exterior*, Vol 34, Num 8, México, August, 1984, pp. 739-750.

SEDUE (Secretaría de Desarrollo UrbanO y Ecología). *Plan Nacional de Vivienda y Desarrollo Urbano (1984-1988)*, 1984.

—*Informe del Programa Nacional de Vivienda*, Abril, 1984.

SPP, Coordinación General de Servicios Nacionales de Estadística, Geografía e Informática. *Censo general de población y vivienda, México*, 1980.
—*Cuadernos de información oportuna de sector salud*, México, 1981.
—*Plan Nacional de Desarrollo, 1983-1988*, 1983.
Ward, Peter, "Mexico City." *Problems and Planning in Third World Cities.* Michael Pacione, ed. London, New York: St. Martin's Press, 1981.

8 Squatters, Oligarchs and Soldiers in San Miguelito, Panama.

by George Priestley

I
Introduction

In the 1960s Latin American economies grew and modernized at unprecedented rates, while their societies increasingly urbanized. Urbanization was accompanied by rapid growth of squatter settlements throughout the major cities in the hemisphere. Politicians and scholars interpreted this mass urban mobilization as both revolutionary and independent of traditional power groups.

It was not too long, however, before both practitioners and academics realized that these so called new urban "marginals" were neither marginalized nor independent of patron-client relations. Rather, they were more or less tied into various types of patron networks and mobilized by regional and/or national power groups.[1] These ties did not emerge automatically. They were the result of concrete historical activities.

In this article I analyze the political mobilization of squatter groups in San Miguelito, Panama by oligarchical governments as well as by a military populist regime. Although I cover most of the postwar period, I will concentrate on the decades of the 1970s and 1980s.

The District of San Miguelito is 51.3 square kilometers and lies northeast of Panama City. In 1960 the community had a population of only 12,975.[2] It jumped to 68,400 in 1970 and 156,611 at the 1980 census. Its population in 1987 is estimated to be just over 240,000. Since in 1986 the nation had 920,000 urban inhabitants, and the Metropolitan Region 800,000, San Miguelito accounted for nearly one third of the region's and the nation's urban population. Only Panama City itself was larger.

Most of San Miguelito's residents are the rural and urban poor who migrate to metropolitan Panama in search of jobs, housing, health and education. They come from every district of the nine provinces of the Republic.[3] They come also from other districts within the metropolitan region. A study conducted by the Ministry of Economic Policy and Planning demonstrated that, of a total of 90,952 migrants who moved from one district to another within the metropolitan region between 1976-1981, San Miguelito received 45,804 while Panama City received only 19,959. Although there were some indications that as of 1985 San Miguelito was sending people to other districts of the metropolitan area, the district still absorbed over 50.3% of all intra-metropolitan migrants.[4]

The massive migration of people toward the metropolitan area is due to the Canal and other important related services in Panama's economy. The metropolitan area produces and consumes most of Panama's resources. Thus, it attracts people from the less dynamic agricultural provinces of Panama.

But San Miguelito neither produces nor consumes very much. It does not have an agricultural or an industrial base. According to a World Bank study for Panama's Ministry of Planning, San Miguelito has 1,682 enterprises, 88% dedicated to commerce and the other 12% dedicated to service and small repair shops. 87% of the 1,682 enterprises are single proprietorships and the other 13% are incorporated. During 1976-1985, there was a 24% increase in the number of small businesses but no significant growth in big business.[5]

Having no significant economic base in their community, San Miguelito's residents work in Panama City and spend most of their meager income there. It is for that reason that San Miguelito is referred to as "la ciudad dormitorio," the dormitory city. Others refer to its population as a "reserve labor" pool for Panama City and environs.

In any event, the district is not economically developed. Its population, with some exceptions, is largely unemployed or under-employed. Its occupation and income structures are inadequate. Its social problems are acute and its ecological situation serious.[6] The economy, unable to provide rural lands or jobs, is equally unable to provide much more than domestic or similar types of jobs for the people of San Miguelito.[7] San Miguelito's unemployment rate has been consistently higher than that of metropolitan Panama. In 1960 San Miguelito had an unemployment rate of 27% and in 1980 it dropped to 13.6%. As we will see later on, the unemployment and income picture in San Miguelito is much worse than the official figures state.[8]

San Miguelito became a political problem in 1968 when the community took to the streets to demonstrate and protest against the military coup that overthrew President Arnulfo Arias on October 11, 1968. Since 1968, the military government or the military-controlled civilian governments of Panama have attempted to solve the most glaring crisis in San Miguelito (housing) while constantly searching for new ways to prevent the community from erupting against the government. But even before 1968, some government attention had been directed to San Miguelito as it emerged as a major squatter community.

In light of the above discussion, the purpose of this article will be threefold. First, it will document the emergence of San Miguelito, its struggles for land, light and water, and the urban problems it reflected and posed for Panama. Second, it will examine the responses of the oligarchy and oligarchical governments to San Miguelito prior to 1968. Finally, it will examine the military government's response in two phases, 1968-1984 and 1984 to the present.

II
San Miguelito Prior to 1968

San Miguelito or, as it was called before 1952, San Miguel Adentro, was sparsely populated prior to the 1940s. During World War II, land invasions in San Miguelito increased as migrants came from the interior provinces in search of jobs. These were joined later in the 1950s and thereafter by the urban slum dwellers of Maranon, Calidonia, Chorrillo and San Miguel. These urban slum dwellers were caught in a metropolitan housing market that, in the 1950s and 1960s, was becoming very expensive as well as tight.[9]

San Miguel Adentro as well as the other *fincas* that make up the District of San Miguelito was owned by a few wealthy Panamanian real estate speculators.[10] Among them are some of Panama's most prominent oligarchical families, such as Domingo Diaz, the Arango family, the Jimenez de Stagg family, and the Goytia and Quijano families. The eight original *fincas* comprised over 32,000 hectares, divided as follows: Santa Elena 1,494; Pan de Azucar, 1,833; Caceres, 1,266; San Miguel Adentro 600; La Pulida, 516; Juan Diaz de Pacora, 25,000; Lucha Franco, 800; Matias Hernandez, 949.

As the migration to San Miguelito continued in the 1950s, these landlords and their government allies became concerned. They were concerned because the number of migrants was increasing, and because they were becoming more organized as they struggled for legal titles to land, and for water and light. The first community organization to emerge was Sociedad San Miguelito Unido, founded in 1952.[11] More organizations followed as the invasions continued. By 1955 there were 200 families and 5 organizations, including the Sociedad de Moradores y Agricultores de San Miguelito, Sociedad Monte Oscuro and Sociedad de la Calle San Miguel.[12] Like Sociedad San Miguelito Unido, these organizations' objectives were land, water, and light.

Between 1952 and 1955 the *finca* Monte Oscuro was the battle scene between landlords, landlords' representatives and local police on the one hand, and the organized community on the other. Members of the Sociedad de Monte Oscuro had to struggle against Pepe Lasso de la Vega, their own President, who supported the landlords, despite being head of the new organization. Unauthorized invaders and builders in Monte Oscuro were attacked and their houses burnt and destroyed by Pepe Lasso de la Vega and the *corregidor* from nearby Pueblo Nuevo.[13] But they did not leave. In 1955 as a result of these struggles and the increasing migration, San Miguelito was given the status of a *regimiento*. This was an administrative sub-division of the *corregimiento* of Pueblo Nuevo, which in turn was a subdivision of the District of Panama.

At first, the landlords and local officials, *regidor* and *corregidor*, confronted the *sociedades*. However by 1958 the National Government was forced to give San Miguelito some place in its budget. In 1959 San Miguelito broke out of its confines and participated in a massive city-wide demonstration against the municipal government of the District of Panama. On February 18, 1959, more than 1200 of San Miguelito's residents joined thousands from other communities in metropolitan Panama in protest against a corrupt and inefficient municipal government.[14] San Miguelito had come of age. It was no longer a loose conglomerate of residents on eight *fincas*. It was a community that had become aware of its unity of purpose, its solidarity with similar communities and its ability to influence governmental decisions.

The decade of the 1960s in Panama was very important economically, socially and politically. The economy grew at an impressive rate of over eight percent per year; commerce and services increased their participation in the economy, but so did construction and industry. Agriculture stagnated. The country experienced significant rural-to-urban migration (mostly to Panama City and San Miguelito) and the industrial and construction work force grew. Politically, the urban poor struggled for a minimum wage and staged massive hunger marches, while students led the fight for complete sovereignty over the Canal Zone. This was a decade of significant capital accumulation, social unrest and political instability.[15]

It was within this context that the residents of San Miguelito struggled for legalization of land titles and access to government services such as water, light, schools and health care. Between 1958 and 1962, San Miguelito, through its organized efforts, was able to force the Liberal government to buy much of the land from the landlords and sell plots to the community. It also pressured the government to respond to their housing needs. In 1959, the Sociedad de Monte Oscuro petitioned the owner of the *finca* to sell the land to the Sociedad. Instead, the owner sold the land to the government of Ernesto de la Guardia for 22.5 cents per square foot. In 1960 the Sociedad pressured the new Liberal President, Roberto Chiari, to sell the land to the settlers and have it administered by the newly created National Housing and Urban Institute (IVU).[16] The IVU had been created by Law 17 of 1958, and its main function became the management and control of San Miguelito.

Recognizing the political importance of San Miguelito, the Liberals moved to upgrade San Miguelito's administrative status from *regimiento* to *corregimiento*. On June 23, 1960, the Municipal Council of Panama City enacted Agreement No. 70, creating the new *corregimiento*. However, it was not until February 1962 that Camilo Saenz was appointed first *corregidor* of San Miguelito.[17] Under Panama's political-administrative code, the *corregidor* is an appointed figure with principally police and judicial functions. This was the first real move on the part of Panama's oligarchical government to set up adequate political mechanisms to influence or control this growing and militant community.[17]

The Chiari government also responded to the community petition for a decent housing program, perhaps also in response to the new Alliance for Progress. In 1961 the IVU set up a program of Mutual Aid (*Ayuda Mutua*). The program was funded by the Inter-American Development Bank, which lent $7.6 million dollars to build housing, streets and other infrastructure. The community was to provide the labor. Four hundred homes were built in 1961. The monthly payments, according to the agreement with the community, were not to exceed $10.00 per month. But the Government was less than candid with the community and its Authentic Association of Mutual Aid. The government had never told them about a six percent interest on the mortgage that the I.D.B. was charging.[18]

In order to announce and implement the six percent mortgage interest, which would have increased the monthly payments significantly, the Liberal Government attempted to divide the Authentic Association of Mutual Aid, and elect someone sympathetic to the government's position. In 1962 the Association held elections, and the government supported Horacio Gomez, who had the support of Belisario Frias—bar owner, noted community activist and now IVU coordinator. The Frias-supported ticket was opposed by Julio Carvajal who was also a noted community activist, whose ticket was called *Reorganización* (Reorganization).[19] The government supported ticket, backed by Frias, lost. San Miguelito had maintained its organizational integrity and was ready to struggle against the six percent mortgage. After several months of demonstrations, the Authentic Association of Mutual Aid agreed to a three percent mortgage interest.[20] The community had not only held its own, but had learned a great deal from the mobilization and organization efforts. For example, the community's outreach included daily radio programs and community meetings in and out of San Miguelito. It was able to mobilize and organize support from Curundu, another squatter community close to the Canal Zone. It elicited and received support from noted lawyers such as Camilo Perez, who acted as the Association's attorney. The Association, in its community meetings, was able to educate community members as to similar tenants' struggles of the past, such as the 1925 Tenants' Strike.[21]

Father Mahon, the Chicago Priests and San Miguelito
As Panama moved into a turbulent 1964, when students and urban masses confronted United States soldiers and Dr. Arnulfo Arias attempted to wrest the presidency from the Liberals, San Miguelito was strengthened not only by its previous struggles but by a new organizing effort by the Catholic Church.

In 1963, the Catholic Church, and in particular Archbishop Msgr. Beckman, urged Father Leo T. Mahon and two other priests to establish an experimental parish in San Miguelito. Father Mahon, a Chicago priest, had had vast experience in programs of consciousness-building or *concientización* in Mexican and Puerto Rican communities in Chicago, Illinois. Father Mahon arrived in Panama in 1963 to set up his consciousness-building program in San Miguelito.[22] By 1965 he had built the church Christ the Redeemer (Cristo Redentor) and formed a number of new *sociedades* such as the Sociedad de Moradores Altos de Paraíso and the Comite de Vivienda (which replaced the dying Authentic Association of Mutual Aid). The Sociedad de Moradores Altos de Paraiso led many invasions and obtained the transfer of squatter residents from Veranillo (a squatter community in front of the National University) to San Miguelito. Over 1000 families received housing as a result of this effort. In 1966, the Committee on Housing (Comité de Vivienda), continuing the efforts of the Authentic Association of Mutual Aid, fought against the IVU for evicting dwellers of the Mutual Aid program. The Comite advanced a rather interesting concept. It reminded the IVU that dwellers could not be evicted since they were co-owners of their homes, not tenants.[23]

Father Mahon's doctrinal and social thoughts are contained in a 1964 document called "The San Miguelito Paper." This document, written by Mahon, was studied, modified and signed by the priests of San Miguelito. The priests saw their principal task as creating a "family," that is, a Christian community. Lesser but important tasks were to form, in the community, a social rather than an individual consciousness; to form a committed people; and to form a community that would fulfill the law, and not merely observe it. In order to achieve these goals a select task force of trained and committed priests would assist and serve as a catalyst for change. They would act as co-creators, thought-provokers, revolutionaries and brothers, not merely as teachers, modernizers, administrators or fathers.

The new thinking within the church, which crystallized in Vatican II (1962-1965) and Medellín (1968), was already evident in Father Mahon's contribution to San Miguelito's social development.[24] Today, there are many radical Christians in Panama who sustain that liberation theology, as outlined and practiced by Father Mahon and the Catholic Church in San Miguelito, preceded and influenced similar, but more radical, versions of this theology in Central America.[25]

Father Mahon set up a *concientización* program to test his approach. Through a set of informal meetings with select community families, the priests studied and reflected on San Miguelito's socio-economic conditions. In these informal sessions, the role of the saints was de-emphasized because, according to one church organizer, "this was a mere image of the traditional political system, where you offer a couple of pesos to someone with *palanca* or pull, and he fixes your license for you. People would burn candles to the saints and feel no responsibility for themselves; they thought the saints would straighten out their problems for them."[26] Obviously, the lay organizers, aided by this new approach, had begun to reject the clientelistic relations that had developed earlier in the decade between the leadership of the Sociedades and the Liberals (e.g., the Liberals' co-optation of Belisario Frias in 1962 to oppose the grassroot ticket.) It also signalled the beginning of a new kind of organization as represented by the Movimiento de Unificación Nacional, Desarrollo y Orientación— MUNDO.

MUNDO grew out of the second phase of the informal sessions held by Mahon and the Chicago priests in 1967. Called *cursillos de iniciación*, these sessions were meant to strengthen the nuclear family and were limited to married couples. In the *cursillos*, discussions were led by laymen about such topics as "Christ as a revolutionary," the true meaning of the sacraments, and the nature of the Christian ideal. Invariably the discussions concluded with an examination of various options for direct action. MUNDO emerged out of these discussions and evaluations.[27]

MUNDO's task was therefore political, that is, to extend the program of *concientización* in order to prepare San Miguelito's Christian leadership to arrive at intelligent, sensible and democratic decisions. MUNDO's strategy for social change in San Miguelito was reformist, gradualist, and not geared to the mass mobilization characteristic of the early 1960s. MUNDO's stagist and reformist approach to change is reflected in a 1967 document entitled *Exposición de Principios*. The document notes that MUNDO's leadership felt that sufficient progress had been made in the area of "individual education" and "family solidification." It was time to address the following: absence or deficiency of public service; unemployment, setting up of local industry; disorganization or insignificance of local commerce and the absence of legitimate politico-administrative structures in San Miguelito. Ramon Hernandez, a MUNDO organizer, said that they eliminated the option of actually forming a political party because of lack of money and political unpreparedness of MUNDO's membership to focus on national issues.[28] It was not too long, however, before MUNDO, Father Mahon and San Miguelito had to respond to the national elections of 1968 and the military coup that followed those elections.

MUNDO's experience, structure and financial situation conditioned its response to the events of 1968 and their aftermath. MUNDO's representatives were selected from all nine sectors of San Miguelito by a general assembly of the community. They were charged with political-civic organizing and with working with governmental agencies such as the IVU. They were to train and sensitize IVU personnel to the needs of San Miguelito's residents. Financing to pay MUNDO's representatives came from three sources: private business firms, IVU and AID.[29] Apparently AID, the U.S. foreign aid agency, channelled its funds through the Community Development Agency which operated as a program inside the Ministry of Labor and Welfare. MUNDO had become closely linked to this agency.[30]

As the 1968 presidential elections drew closer, politicians inundated San Miguelito in search of "bloc" votes, obtained through deals with political brokers who would in turn deliver the votes of their constituencies. Ramon Hernandez said, "Since we (MUNDO) represented leadership in the community, both sides tried to use us. They offered to give us certain things if the people voted for them. When we refused to go along, the politicians withdrew all their financial support and we found ourselves without enough money to continue our work. So in order to sustain our families, we took jobs with the Church (San Miguelito parish) or sought work somewhere else."[31]

Evidently MUNDO and the church remained outside of the clientele network in the 1968 elections. But how effective was this tactic given the fact that AID monies were tied to "strings" and were drying up, and that IVU's monies and private enterprise monies were also insufficient and equally tied to "strings"? Although Herasto Reyes, author of San Miguelito's history, is quite sympathetic to Mahon and MUNDO, he feels that their emphasis on perfecting man and *then* perfecting society was ill-conceived and dangerous for San Miguelito's development.[32]

III
San Miguelito and the 1968 Coup

In spite of San Miguelito's political weakness during the 1960s, its growth and struggles were part of a more general socio-political development that led to the collapse of the Liberal oligarchical order. The collapse of the oligarchy, and the 1968 military coup, were due to four developments in the 1960s. First of all, economic growth in the 1960s, based on a policy of import substitution, did not bring quick benefits to the majority of the Panamanian people. Second, the popular movement was again radicalized in response to the economic situation: workers and the urban masses mounted a struggle for employment and a $0.40 minimum wage. Third, the middle class, led by student organizations, stepped up the struggle for sovereignty over the Canal Zone. And fourth, the oligarchy's inability to incorporate the new urban masses, institute needed reforms or secure the decolonization of the Canal Zone caused it to be seriously split. This split was evidenced in the 1968 elections. The military, however, moved against President-elect Arnulfo Arias only when it was evident that Dr. Arias was about to reshuffle the hierarchy of the National Guard (the military).[33]

Immediately after the overthrow of President Arias, MUNDO, the church and their constituents openly opposed the military coup of October 11, 1968. MUNDO issued a position paper called, "The Fourth Line" ("La Cuarta Linea"). "The Fourth Line" opposed Dr. Arnulfo Arias, (Panamenista Party and President-elect), David Samudio, presidential candidate for the Liberal Party, and the military. The document read, "We do not want to be subordinated to the military; we will not accept tyranny in any form, for tyrannies are the detractors of our liberty and progress."[34]

MUNDO and Father Mahon led several demonstrations to protest the military coup. The demonstrators were primarily San Miguelito's residents, joined by university students. The police did not use force to break up the demonstrations, which were primarily non-violent. However, the military forced a dialogue with the demonstrators by continuously containing the march and reducing its numbers. At their highest point, the demonstrations had reached 3,000 people.[35]

Omar Torrijos, one of the leaders of the coup, who was still sharing power with other military figures, delegated Lic. Materno Vasquez and Carlos Lopez Guevara to open a dialogue with the leaders of San Miguelito. Materno Vasquez, representing Torrijos' left-wing alliance, had recently been appointed as Secretary to the Office of the President. Lopez Guevara, an eminent international jurist and former Minister of Foreign Affairs, represented Torrijos' right wing. Although Lopez Guevara turned against the Torrijos regime in the late

1970s, for most of the 1970s he served as a member of the 1977 canal negotiating team. Torrijos had not sent lightweights to meet with San Miguelito's leadership.

Position papers and demonstrations notwithstanding, when the Torrijos-led government spokesmen entered into direct dialogue with leaders of San Miguelito, the main point of discussion was not restoration of individual freedom for all citizens or housing, but rather the creation of an experimental District in San Miguelito. This agenda was politically dependent, since individual freedoms were out of the question and housing was too expensive.

San Miguelito's move from *regimiento* to *corregimiento* to Special District in fewer than fifteen years was a dramatic and welcome development for the original squatters of the 1950s. Special District status meant that San Miguelito would no longer depend on the District of Panama (Panama City) for essential services, but rather could become fiscally solvent by acquiring constitutional rights to raise taxes and borrow monies.[36] San Miguelito's aspiration for fiscal independence and solvency never materialized, however.

In agreeing to the experimental District in San Miguelito, Torrijos and the military had not only neutralized the government's most vocal urban opposition, but gained an opportunity to put in practice the concept of *Junta-Pueblo-Gobierno*. At best, the concept, which was coined by the military, meant military rule with local popular participation. At worst, it meant a military control of San Miguelito by way of a new mode of state-local community articulation.[37] This new articulation would replace the traditional clientele politics whereby community leaders, as brokers, would relate to individual politicians or bureaucrats.

The 1969-1972 Period

The new District of San Miguelito was legally created by Decree 258 of July 1970, a few months after Torrijos consolidated his personal political power. It became a vehicle for the military to contain and control San Miguelito's church directed movement. The process of containing and controlling San Miguelito was and still is a difficult one. The process responded to correlation of political and economic forces both inside and outside the District.

The military was not sponsoring radical or revolutionary changes. It was doing whatever was necessary to consolidate its rule and implement necessary reforms by way of a new alliance which included students, labor, fractions of capital and the Partido del Pueblo (Panama's Communist Party). As became evident between 1969 and 1972, the military was not so much interested in encouraging genuine autonomous local participatory structures as it was in creating new constitutional structures, including a National Assembly of 505 community representatives, to legitimize its rule. New bureaucratic structures such as the General Directorate for Community Development (DIGEDECOM) were also set up.

DIGEDECOM was created by Cabinet Decree on June 3, 1969. Its purpose was to supervise and direct community development programs of the national government. DIGEDECOM's predecessor was the above mentioned AID sponsored Office of Community Development which operated out of the Labor Ministry.[38] Once DIGEDECOM was established, preparation for self rule under government supervision was well under way. Former members of MUNDO were hired as DIGEDECOM employees in San Miguelito, while others were hired as organizers by a now solvent MUNDO. The project for a Special District, designed by these two agencies, was ready for implementation by December of 1969.

On December 7, 1969, Father Mahon sent a memorandum to General Torrijos urging the general to set up a special committee to implement the plan. In the memorandum Mahon called on Torrijos to avoid any semblance of paternalism, called on the General to ensure effective community participation, and suggested that Jose Arrocha, Rafael Medina and Eric De Leon be assigned to the implementation committee. Arrocha and Medina worked for DIGEDECOM and De Leon worked in the Planning Office of the Presidency. All three, however, were former cursillistas and personal confidants of Father Mahon. Mahon's request was promptly granted by Torrijos.[39]

Torrijos survived a counter-coup on December 16, 1969. On January 25, 1970 he moved quickly to consolidate control over the implementation of governing and administrative structures in the new district. He appointed Manuel Balbino Moreno, at the time Comptroller General of the Republic, as National Coordinator of DIGEDECOM with special powers to act in San Miguelito. MUNDO and Mahon had hoped for an elected mayor for the new district. Moreno insisted that the mayor be appointed by the Ministry of Government and Justice. Until 1984, in Panama's politico-administrative structure, the appointed mayor was subordinated to the governor of his/her respective province and responsible for police matters in his/her jurisdiction. According to articles 13 and 14 of Cabinet Decree 258 of July 30, 1969, the mayor also presides over the Municipal Council; legally represents the municipality; submits budgets of income and expenses to the council; submits proposals for creating municipal enterprises for economic and industrial development; submits for the consideration of the Community Assembly proposed agreements to assess taxes, contributions, rents, rights and rates, to cover the cost of administration and municipal services; and promotes urban development in accordance with scientific planning. It is clear that much of the municipal developmental functions came from MUNDO and Mahon. The Community Assembly structure, the heart of popular participation in the district, also came from MUNDO and Mahon.

Articles 5 through 9 of Cabinet Decree 258 of July 30, 1969 deal with the structure of the new Community Assembly. Basically, the district was divided into 68 sectors and each sector would elect a person to the Assembly, the most representative body of the district. On the other hand the Municipal Council, the real legislative body, would consist of 15 councilmen/women, each representing or chosen by 4 sectors.

Although the Municipal Administration consisted of the Community Assembly, the Municipal Council and the mayor, there was a great concentration of power in the office of the mayor. MUNDO and Mahon knew this. Torrijos knew it too. Both sides insisted on having a say as to who would be the first mayor. A compromise was worked out when both sides agreed that Mahon would submit three names from which Torrijos would select one. Mahon's first choice, Paulino Salazar, was chosen by Torrijos. But Torrijos had established a precedent of appointing the mayor and hence holding the right to remove him/her.

There is no doubt that Torrijos was aware of the urban nightmare that San Miguelito was becoming, that is, a receptacle for tens of thousands of migrants who were victims of existing social relations in Panama and who were in search of the basic necessities of life: food, housing, health care and education. Paulino Salazar, an engineer and businessman, seemed capable of organizing the government's resources to solve these problems. On the other hand, there is no doubt that Torrijos was equally insistent in bringing San Miguelito into a new and subordinate relation to the State. He had hoped Salazar would understand that. As discussed below, Salazar did not, and was summarily removed.

Salazar's removal from office was also, in part, a result of general tensions between Torrijos and the Church.[40] It was further facilitated by a schism in San Miguelito between those *sociedades* leaders who yearned for the old clientele relation and those leaders committed to the new municipal structures. A case in point is the position of the president of a sector called *Silos del Ife*. At a community meeting, he said,

The problem is that the streets in this community are in terrible condition. In the past, we used to contact the Ministry of Pubic Works and they would send us a road grader and some materials. We would put in the rest of the materials and manpower. In September 1970, we sent a letter to the Ministry in which we requested a list of materials, including cement, iron, rods, gravel, etc. Everything was approved, but we heard nothing more from them. So we wrote again in January of 1971, and we received a letter dated January 29, saying that, 'in accordance with the Cabinet Decree creating the District of San Miguelito, all requests for materials should be channeled through the mayor's office.' This society has worked with the Municipal Government from the start. We have among us three members of the Area Council, including Sr. Orocu who is also a member of the Municipal Council. But, in October of 1970, we tried to get those materials through the municipality and we were told that funds were not yet budgeted for public works. One of my friends in the Ministry is always asking me why the Municipality is not giving us these things. I do not know what to say to him.[41]

Obviously such leaders were unhappy about not having direct access to the various national ministries and the budgeting process of the new municipality. Before Decree 258, there was no area council which superseded the *sociedades,* there was no Municipal Council and no mayor to negotiate with. The presidents of the societies had had direct contacts with the ministries. Decree 258 ended that situation, and many *sociedades* were discontented.

The presidents of the *sociedades* became allies of Torrijos as state and church relations worsened in the summer of 1971. They must have known that Torrijos intended to create five new *corregimientos* and return some local control to the *sociedades* which would, in conjunction with the military and the Partido del Pueblo, elect and control the representatives of the *corregimientos* of San Miguelito. In the meantime, they had to await the outcome of church-state conflict, which came to a head in July. An open-air mass was held on July 18 at *Iglesia del Carmen*, the church of the very rich. Msgr. MacGrath organized a demonstration of 15,000 people. The Torrijos regime played down the demonstration, but was quick to point out that many oligarchical politicians were among the front line marchers. Torrijos argued that the oligarchy was utilizing the church's demonstration to weaken the government's negotiating position with the United States over the Canal issue. Torrijos knew that to effectively negotiate a new canal policy with the United States, he had to forge some kind of national unity. The Gallegos case and the church's response were clearly endangering that unity. (Father Hector Gallegos disappeared in June 1971. The church blamed the military.) And so Torrijos responded by planning a massive rally on October 11 in celebration of the third anniversary of the coup.

At this important juncture, as Torrijos forged the basis for the legitimacy of the military government and a new canal policy, he required complete cooperation/subordination of all politico-administrative agencies, including the newly created District of San Miguelito. Torrijos made it known that all agencies should allocate resources toward the planning of the mass rally on October 11. It was at this point that Salazar, San Miguelito's mayor, found that he could not adhere to Torrijos' mandate. He was promptly removed, and replaced by José Arrocha. Arrocha, an employee of DIGEDECOM, was a former director of MUNDO and a member of the organizing committee of the San Miguelito Plan. Belisario Frias, who previously had served in the Liberal government of Roberto Chiari, was appointed Assistant Mayor. Frias had also been one of the staunchest opponents of the San Miguelito Plan in so far as that plan had infringed on the powers of the *sociedades*. On October 11, 1971, the San Miguelito community, alongside 200,000 other Panamanians, turned out at the Plaza Cinco de Mayo to demonstrate support for the military regime of Omar Torrijos and to support the regime's anti-colonial canal policy.

At the national level, the correlation of political forces had changed in favor of Torrijos and the military. In San Miguelito there was a similar change as the military alliance succeeded Mahon, MUNDO and the Church. As Eric de Leon commented in a 1973 interview, "the Special District as we knew it is dead."[42] The military had successfully dealt with the San Miguelito challenge. It co-opted some of its leaders, isolated others and abrogated important structures, replacing them with new ones, such as the *representantes de corregimientos*, that were more amenable to the requirements of the regime.[43]

In order to make everything nice and legal, that is to legally abolish San Miguelito's pre-existing democratic structures (Community Assembly and Area Council), the regime approved article 161 of Law 106 of October 1973. Article 161 abolished articles 4 through 32 of Cabinet Decree of July 30, 1970. The Community Assembly and Area Council were replaced by new participatory structures.

San Miguelito's experiment in local popular participation served the regime as a model for creating the 505 local participatory bodies (Juntas Comunales) based on the geographic-administrative unit called the *corregimiento*. Together the 505 representatives formed the National Assembly of Community Representatives. San Miguelito's five *corregimientos*, like the other 500 nationwide, were to become important structures of participation, albeit completely and systemically linked to the new military regime.

As a result of the new 1972 Constitution, whereby 505 local representatives governed locally (many on behalf of the military), San Miguelito obtained five representatives, one for each of its five *corregimientos*: Amelia Denis de Icaza, Mateo Iturralde, Victoriano Lorenzo, Domingo Espinar and Belisario Porras. Almost all of the local representatives elected in 1972 and 1978 to these *corregimientos* were either directly related to the military or the Partido del Pueblo. Ali Nunez of the Partido del Pueblo was elected representative of corregimiento Belisario Porras in 1972 and again in 1978. The military and its junior partner, Partido del Pueblo, governed San Miguelito for the period 1972-1984.

IV
San Miguelito Under Military Rule 1973-1984

This experiment in popular participation under a consolidated military regime failed. It did not fail because of ill intention or bad faith. An inconsistent mix of paternalism and participation, it was designed to fail.

Housing Development
During the decade of the 1970s the military government of General Omar Torrijos invested a great deal of money on human and physical infrastructure. Massive public spending and investment were part of Torrijos' strategy of gaining political legitimacy for military rule and for reorganizing a new bourgeois hegemony, and as we saw earlier, San Miguelito was important in forging the new legitimacy.[44] Beginning in 1973, the military attacked the most critical problem in San Miguelito: housing.

Between 1960 and 1970 San Miguelito had grown by 470%, and it grew by another 170% between 1970 and 1980. In spite of the fact that General Torrijos had approved and had implemented a progressive land reform program, rural-to-urban migration in Panama increased significantly.[45]

With this rapid growth, San Miguelito developed many urban problems. Among these were a persistent housing shortage and highly inadequate housing, sewage, water and lighting facilities. George Kourany, the current chief adviser to the Minister of Housing, estimated that in 1984 there was a national housing deficit of 183,000 units. Of this figure, 63,000 units were lacking in Panama City and San Miguelito.[46] As a result of this housing shortage in Panama City, old as well as new migrants continued to pour into San Miguelito and especially into the *corregimiento* of Belisario Porras.[47]

In order to meet this severe urban crisis, the Torrijos government begun an aggressive housing and urbanization program in San Miguelito. During the decade of the 1970s, the military regime invested millions of dollars to rehabilitate dilapidated houses and to build new ones. Emphasis was placed on poor communities like Cerro Batea, Santa Librada, Torrijos-Carter and Roberto Duran. But some middle class communities within San Miguelito were also built or subsidized, especially for members of the expanding bureaucracy. La Pulida, Los Andes and El Bosque are the better known ones. Private contractors and builders also invested in some lower-middle and middle class housing, where land was still privately owned. San Antonio and Cerro Viento are cases in point.

Through IVU, and its successor, the Ministry of Housing (MIVI), the national government invested over $82 million in San Miguelito from 1961 through 1986. The investment, 32% of the national social investment budget, has not only been spent on housing. In order to comply with IMF recommendations made in the early 1980s, the government de-emphasized the building of housing and emphasized acquisition, preparation of lots, installation of sewage and water and the lending of building materials to qualified residents.[48]

On balance, the aggressive housing program that the military government undertook in the 1970s in San Miguelito has contained the housing crisis in this community. But wider urban problems remained, as will be seen.

Local Government

For most of the 1970s the military-led populist coalition held firm control of Panama's political process. The coalition, however, began to show signs of weakness as early as late 1977, just after the signing of the Carter-Torrijos treaties. For the next seven years, the populist coalition was unable to hold on to power. Troubled by bad economic performance, renewed social conflicts between labor and capital and by the so-called 'democratic opening,' which was characterized by a brief return of the military to the barracks, the populist coalition unraveled as the dominant political and economic groups sought a new realignment of power.[49]

In San Miguelito, the military and the Partido del Pueblo shared the administration of the District until 1984. The appointed or elected officials of the district were cadres either of the military or the Partido del Pueblo. After defeating MUNDO, Father Mahon and the non-governmental progressives in San

Miguelito, the government coalition appointed several mayors and elected a clear majority of the district's Community Representatives (*representantes de corregimiento*).

The most visible and important of these representatives was Ali Nunez, who was closely linked to both the Communist Party and the military. Ali Nunez was elected in 1972 and again in 1978 as the representative of the corregimiento of Belisario Porras in San Miguelito. As representative of the largest and most problematic of the five *corregimientos* of San Miguelito, he was quite important to the military.

In 1973 the military decided to attack the housing problems of Samaria in the *corregimiento* of Belisario Porras. Together with AID, the government launched Proyecto Samaria, or PROSA. More than a construction project, PROSA, at a cost of over $5 million, began to address the problems of legalization, surveying of lots, and rehabilitation of lands in Samaria. The project installed some water and sewage in Nuevo Vernaillo, which is also in Samaria. The government claims that over 5000 families benefited directly or indirectly from the project.[50]

PROSA was important in at least two ways. First, it demonstrated the willingness of the military-led populist coalition to meet some of the housing needs of an important district in the metropolitan area. Secondly, it gave an important administrative role to Ali Nunez as the president of the Commmunity Board (Junta Comunal) of the *corregimiento* of Belisario Porras.[51]

The Community Board and the district were charged by the Catholics with malfeasance, corruption and inefficiency. Moreover, Ali Nunez and the Board had had many difficulties with members of the Mahon group and the Health Committee of Samaria. Although the Junta Comunal-Health Committee conflict was not unique to San Miguelito, in Samaria its resolution was made difficult by the church-state controversy. According to Father Karamenitis of Samaria, Ali Nunez assumed a bitter and negative attitude toward the church. Karamenitis said that in 1973 Nunez took over the locale of the Health Committee of Samaria and converted it for his personal and political use.[52]

It is within this context of alleged corruption and persistent conflict between Nunez and those related to the church that members of the Christian Base movement stormed the office of the mayor of San Miguelito and took it over, in the so-called "Cabildazo" of 1974. They were soon dispersed, and not until 1984, when Father Karamenitis and members of his parish recovered their locale from Ali Nunez, did the Christian movement again take militant action in San Miguelito. Realizing the inadequacy of both the local representative, who was also President of the Community Board, and the mayor in handling the Samaria situation, General Torrijos appointed a High Commission to oversee the resource and crisis management of San Miguelito.[53] He appointed Colonel Ruben Paredes as the coordinator of the High Commission of San Miguelito, but the day to day operation of the Commission was carried out by Mayor A. Cedeño,

Nilson Espino and Samuel Gutierrez. Espino and Gutierrez, both respected professionals, brought credibility to the Commission. Between 1974 and 1980 the High Commission was the de facto municipal authority in San Miguelito. It coordinated the efforts of all National Government and Autonomous Agencies and directly administered the Urban Development Program of San Miguelito, DUISMI.

DUISMI was the most ambitious urban program undertaken by the military. It was conceived as an integral response to San Miguelito's problems. The architects of the program stated that the objective was not only to provide San Miguelito with adequate infrastructure (aqueducts, sewage, electrification, streets, sidewalks and housing) but also to reduce unemployment by providing construction jobs and aiding small enterprises.[54] The planning and design of DUISMI began in 1975, and were implemented from 1978 through 1981. The investment was $18,896,800. AID contributed 80% and the National Government 20%. By all accounts, the project failed. Its failure has been blamed on bad planning, lack of community participation and corruption in high places.[55]

At the First Seminar on Urban Problems in San Miguelito, held in Jaunary 1987, the representative of the Ministry of Political Economy and Planning said that DUISMI had failed because of poor coordination and lack of community cooperation. The representative said that in spite of the heavy governmental investment in the district, the effects were not felt. As a result, she continued, the government had decided to discontinue the investment plan and instead to draw up a priority plan to serve the truly needy.[56] In the discussion that followed it became evident that many residents continued to use latrines and communal water systems because the cost of gaining access to the sewage and water provided by DUISMI was too high. The cost of access to the sewage system alone was $1,000.00. Given the socio-economic profile of San Miguelito, it is hardly surprising that many residents could not afford the infrastructure provided for them.

A more serious charge against the High Commission's administration of DUISMI was that it was a source of corruption, and that it usurped the legitimate functions of the municipality of San Miguelito. Allegations of military and governmental corruption in the administration of DUISMI have not been corroborated. However, given the scandalous abuse of the Social Security System by high governmental officials in the 1980s, one cannot entirely discount the allegations. On the other hand, the charges that the High Commission usurped the powers of the municipal authorities should be put in context. The district of San Miguelito was created by the military for political as well as for administrative purposes. Since the defeat of Mahon, MUNDO and their followers, San Miguelito had been ruled from above and from outside: by the General Directorate of Community Development (DIGEDECOM), the military and the High Commission, but not by the municipal authorities.

V
San Miguelito and the 1984 Elections

In 1984, the people of San Miguelito voted to change this situation. As a result of the so-called democratic opening, the military regime decided to hold national and municipal elections in 1984. It was the first time since 1968 that the Panamanian people were given the right to select their national and local leaders through direct and secret ballots. At this point, the local Community Boards were severely weakened, the local representatives were replaced by nationally elected legislators, and the National Assembly of Community Representatives was replaced by a national legislature.

Ironically, the two coalitions that contested the elections, the National Democratic Union (UNADE) and the Democratic Opposition Alliance (ADO), had much in common with the coalitions that competed in the 1968 elections.[57] In spite of the limited choice offered by two opposing coalitions, Panamanians went to the polls in May and June 1984 to elect national and municipal officers. Ardito Barletta, presidential candidate of UNADE, was elected in what everyone agreed was a fraudulent election. (He was removed by the military in November 1985.)[58] In San Miguelito, the Ardito Barletta ticket lost by 10,000 votes and in the municipal elections the military-backed coalition, UNADE, had to settle for a draw. UNADE captured all five *corregimientos* in San Miguelito; but of the five legislative seats allocated to San Miguelito, UNADE captured only three. Although a UNADE member, Balbina Herrera De Perinan, won the mayoral race, the coalition did not in fact support her.[59]

In order to understand the electoral and extra-coalition conflict, some background on the parties is needed. The Democratic Revolutionary Party (PRD) was created by General Omar Torrijos in 1978 to serve as a mass party linked to the military. It was to be the new source of legitimacy for military rule. While Torrijos was alive, the party did well, but soon after Torrijos' death in 1981, the party succumbed to internal squabbles. By 1982 a realignment of political forces had moved the party closer to the right of the political spectrum, as it sought agreements with traditional parties such as the Liberal Party, the Labor-Agrarian Party (PALA) and other lesser groups. These parties together presented candidates as UNADE in 1984. In the process, the PRD distanced itself from its old ally, the Partido del Pueblo, and attempted to discipline its left wing.

The left wing of the PRD is led by the so-called *Tendencia*. The *Tendencia* is comprised of the student leadership that supported Torrijos as early as 1971. In 1974, it broke with the Partido del Pueblo and became the left wing of the military-sponsored populist movement. Along with the labor movement and the agricultural reform sector (Confederación de Asentamientos), the *Tendencia* was most important to Torrijos. After his death in 1981 the *Tendencia* had to renegotiate its status within the PRD with the new military leaders. As part of this negotiation, the military demanded electoral support from the *Tendencia* for its candidate in the 1984 San Miguelito mayoral election.

The national leadership of the *Tendencia* was unable to persuade its regional cadres to go along with the military's request. Instead, the San Miguelito section of the *Tendencia* prevailed within the PRD and nominated Balbina Herrera de Perinan, a young left-of-center feminist. (Balbina was a national figure and regional leader of FENAMUDE, a feminist movement connected to the Torrijos process.)Against all odds, Balbina defeated the military's candidate for the PRD's nomination. On June 10, 1984, the people of San Miguelito elected Balbina Herrera de Perinan as their first popularly elected Mayor. Her deputy mayor, Osvaldo Castro Rodriguez, apparently had the support of the military.

Why did Balbina Herrera de Perinan not receive the support of her party— the Democratic Revolutionary Party? Why after winning the mayoralty, did both the PRD and the military remain hostile to her? Can she win in 1989? These are some of the questions that need to be addressed if San Miguelito's political and developmental future is to be comprehended.

Although Balbina Herrera de Perinan was elected by a splinter group of the *Tendencia*, neither the mayor nor her supporters have broken away from the PRD. They operate, without much success, as an independent faction of the *Tendencia* within the PRD. The mayor has been unable to gain the support of the two PRD legislators. Neither Jorge Simmons nor "Lucho" Gomez has been of much help to the mayor in obtaining economic and political support for the district. On the contrary, Lucho Gomez, also of the *Tendencia*, has distanced himself from the mayor on a number of important issues. He has not supported her demand for an emergency meeting of the Council of State (all Cabinet Ministers) to address the district's problems and he has not supported her request for higher budget allocations or even for allocations that have been made but not paid to the district.[60]

Without the necessary resources, the mayor has not been able to adequately address any of San Miguelito's historical problems. Unemployment, health care, juvenile delinquency, garbage collection, housing and transportation are problems that are very much present in San Miguelito.

While Balbina de Perinan struggles to obtain a hearing in San Miguelito with the National Council of State (the Cabinet), Lucho Gomez seems to favor a formula closer akin to the erstwhile High Commission of San Miguelito. Such a commission might allow Lucho Gomez and other legislators from San Miguelito to shine in the national limelight, but it would certainly dim the relative autonomy that the district obtained in 1984.

Some high officials in the district of San Miguelito feel that the military has a strategy geared to reducing the political space of the district. They say that there are several elements to that strategy. Politically, the government and the military refuse to call a meeting of the Council of State and instead are sending out feelers toward reconstituting another High Commission on San Miguelito. Economically, the national government has reduced the municipal budget of San Miguelito from $1.6 million dollars to $1.2 million dollars and the Ministry of Planning has withheld a portion of the district's investment budget. Ideologically, the mayor has been and continues to be depicted in the newspapers and on the walls of San Miguelito as a thief.[61]

Whether or not there is a strategy to reduce the political space of the present municipal administration, there is little cooperation between the mayor's office and the elected PRD legislators. For two consecutive years, the municipal budget has been reduced by $300,000 or more, and $500,000 of its 1986 investment budget is being held up by the Ministry of Planning. (The ministry claims that the municipality has not fulfilled AID guidelines and hence the hold.)[62] There are daily attacks against the mayor in the government-controlled dailies, and there are graffiti strategically located within the district that depict the mayor unfavorably. Whether they are part of a design or not, these factors have immobilized the municipal administration and have kept it from organizing the necessary resources to solve the district's problems.

Looking ahead to 1989, the mayor defined 1987 as the year for action. Admonishing the national government (and the military), she predicted that if action is not taken to solve San Miguelito's problems, the government's presidential candidate will lose in San Miguelito by more than 10,000 votes.[63] Admonitions notwithstanding, Mayor Balbina Herrera Perinan and her team still have to devise an electoral strategy for 1989. As of January 1987 such a strategy was glaringly absent.

VI
Concluding Remarks

In 1987, San Miguelito is very different from what it was in 1960. The district not only increased its population from 12,000 to over 244,000 inhabitants, but many of its newer communities, and a few of its older ones, have a majority of middle income residents. This new demographic and economic development makes it difficult to duplicate the successful mobilization of the 1950s and 1960s.

Moreover, after nearly twenty years of military rule and military inspired administration, San Miguelito's structures of autonomous local participation have been replaced either by Community Boards, quasi-administrative bodies, or by new legislative and municipal structures. In addition to these structures, which stifle rather than encourage genuine political participation, the military has created a special military zone and various civic action programs in the district, thereby increasing its influence and control in the community.

At the same time, the mutual benefit community organizations, known as *sociedades*, and the Christian-based groups have all but disappeared. In 1977, 1979 and 1981, the Christian-based groups re-emerged briefly in the district to participate in the Carter-Torrijos treaty debates and to build bridges of solidarity with the peoples of Nicaragua and El Salvador. These efforts, although important, were short-lived. And in the absence of a city-wide or nationwide coherent popular movement, San Miguelito in the 1980s has remained within the orbit of the military and its civilian creation, the Revolutionary Democratic Party.

The question remains as to whether San Miguelito can break out of the orbit of the military. If it does, would it enter the orbit of the right-wing opposition led by the forces of former President Arnulfo Arias, as the Christian Democratic Party has nationally? Or is there a third option? It is my contention that San Miguelito, in the 1980s and beyond, will play an important role in protest as well as electoral politics. It is no longer marginal to the politics of Panama City; its politics and that of the city are one. This fact becomes obvious when one realizes that the city, moving and growing north and east, has practically merged into the District of San Miguelito. Its future growth will be within the district itself and in the *areas revertidas*, (lands that the U.S. returned to Panama by virtue of the Carter-Torrijos treaty) just south of it.

Up until the mid 1960s, San Miguelito was predominantly a squatter community. Its residents were either squatting on privately owned land or had been the recipients of land and/or housing from IVU or MIVI. In 1987, housing in San Miguelito is 50% formal (housing built on legalized land, according to specifications and building codes) and 50% informal. However, in the last two years, fourteen new squatter communities have appeared. There are over 20,000 persons in these new communities, and most of their houses are completely improvised. Those that are on terrain under 50 meters above sea level are able to access water from nearby government-built communities like Torrijos Carter and Roberto Duran.[64]

Just beyond these new squatter settlements are various buffers to the east and north in the *corregimiento* of Domingo Espinar. To prevent the spread of squatter communities into the vacant lands of Domingo Espinar, land owners have adopted a dual strategy. They have paid armed men to prevent further incursions, and they have begun to build moderately priced one family homes. Such is the case of Villa Lucre in the *corregimiento* of Domingo Espinar.

There is very little in the way of public-owned land in San Miguelito. The municipality owns almost no land; the National Mortgage Bank owns a small percentage and the balance belongs to private owners. And since the municipality has virtually no land, its role in the future development of San Miguelito will be restricted. Unless the district obtains land or the necessary resources with which to plan the development of the district, the main players in its development will be land developers, the military, the national government and, if they are organized, the new urban squatters.

Given the rate of invasions, and given that the district has little public lands for housing, schools, parks and so on, how much of San Miguelito is left for development? How much does it cost? And what are the government's projections? Of the five *corregimientos*, Domingo Espinar is the only one where quick, easy and relatively inexpensive urban projects could be built.[65] Domingo Espinar runs along the Tocumen highway and borders to the east with the *corregimiento* of Pedregal; it has over 40% of the land of San Miguelito. At $40 a square foot, it is not as expensive as El Bosque, where land sells for $80 a square foot, but not as inexpensive as Belisario Porras, where land sells for $20 a square foot.

Belisario Porras has 21 square kilometers, of which 11 sq. km. are occupied (6.5 sq. km. are formal and 4.5 sq. km are informal); Domingo Espinar has 24.2 sq. km. of which only 7 sq. km. are occupied (5 sq. km. formal and 2 sq. km. squatter or informal). The development of the unoccupied lands in this *corregimiento* depends on the opening of the proposed "North Corridor" highway. Panamanian government plans for this highway appear in ESTAMPA, the Japanese transportation feasibility study of metropolitan Panama. While there are those who view the project as necessary to ease the metropolitan traffic burden, especially at important bottlenecks in San Miguelito, there are others who feel that the highway will unlock Domingo Espinar's lands for development. They say that this is part of a continuing process of land valorization that benefits the very rich.

Meanwhile, with the exception of a few middle class communities, San Miguelito still has acute problems of unemployment, under-employment, transportation, recreation, public services, medical services, shopping centers and other requirements for proper urbanization. For example, the 1981 ESTAMPA study on urban transportation stated that San Miguelito lacked secondary roads within the confines of the district. This, of course, makes it very difficult to move from one community to another within the district.

There are no hospitals, no libraries and no parks in the district. (The wife of a former president donated a park in 1978. But no provision was made for its upkeep, and the park now serves as a receptacle for garbage.[66]) And although the relatively new middle-class communities of El Bosque, Los Andes, La Pulida and San Antonio have benefited from the aggressive building programs of the 1970s, other early-1980s communities such as Samaria, San Isidro, Torrijos-Carter and Roberto Duran still have severe housing, employment and other infrastructural problems.

The newer squatter settlements are in worse shape. La Felicidad, General Noriega and La Paz are replicas of the earlier squatter communities of Pan de Azucar, San Miguel Adentro, Ojo de Agua and Monte Oscuro. Houses, mostly made from inadequate and inferior materials, are arranged randomly and sometimes dangerously along trails, streets and hilltops. And while the residents of these squatter communities "steal" water and light from now legalized communities such as Torrijos-Carter, they lack sewers, latrines, roads, walkways and garbage disposals. Until the national government, the National Defense Force, the District of Panama and the District of San Miguelito address the problems of these newer and even older migrants, San Miguelito remains at best a severe urban dilemma and at worst an urban powder keg.

As indicated by the ESTAMPA Study, San Miguelito and the former Canal Zone are central to Panama's urban development. Whether San Miguelito will continue to develop as an option for squatters or for the middle class will depend on a number of economic and political factors. Above all, it will depend on who controls San Miguelito. So far, the military, the PRD and the Partido del Pueblo have failed to institutionalize control over the district; nevertheless, they have succeeded in preventing the rise of a progressive and popular alternative.

Notes

I extend special thanks to Segundo Pantoja, my research assistant and graduate student of Latin American Studies at Queens College, who accompanied me to San Miguelito in January 1987. Matthew Edel, chair of Urban Studies at Queens College urged me to write the essay and patiently edited various drafts. In Panama I am indebted to many people, especially those in the various *ministerios* who shared their data and insights with me. However, special thanks goes to the small but able team of professionals who staff the Mayor's office in San Miguelito.

1. For early studies, see David Collier, *Squatters and Oligarchs: Authoritarian Rule and Policy Change in Peru*, Baltimore, Johns Hopkins University Press, 1976, and Wayne A. Cornelius, *Politics and the Migrant Poor in Mexico City*, Stanford University Press, 1975. For a later work that documents clientele relations and electoral politics in Ecuador, see Amparo Menéndez-Carrión, *La Conquista del voto: De Velasco a Roldós*, Quito, Corporación Editora Nacional, 1986, and lastly for a provocative and brilliant thematical effort, which examines the breadth of relationships between urban squatter communities and power groups, see Manuel Castells, *Crísis urbana y cambio social*, Mexico City, Siglo XXI, 1981.

2. *Censos Nacionales de 1980*, Vol. VII Sectores Censales de los Distritos de Panamá, San Miguelito y Colón. p. 131.

3. Districts of Colón, Chagres, Donoso, Portobelo, Santa Isabel, Taboga, Arraiján, Capira, Chame, Chepo, Chorrera, Panama, San Carlos, Balboa and San Miguelito.

4. Figures from Mr. Dorado, World Bank Consultant to the Ministry of Planning. See interview with Pablo Vivar, of Ministry of Planning and Economic Policy, 1-20-87, Planificación.

5. Dr. Carlos Dorado paper read at the "Primer Encuentro de Problemas Urbanos—San Miguelito/1987" January 6-10, 1987, San Miguelito, Panama.

6. See Dr. Carlos Dorado, *op. cit.*

7. See George Kourany, Executive Advisor to the Minister of Housing in "Proyecciones San Miguelito," unpublished paper, 1987, p. 6.

8. Of a population of 1,831,339 in 1980, Panama Province had 831,048, Panama City 499,055 and San Miguelito 156,611. *Censos Nacionales de Población p. 15*. Also, in 1984 the metropolitan region provided 50% of new jobs, but in 1985 it

provided only 10% of new jobs while the rest of the country provided 90% of new jobs in the same year. This dramatic reversal is due to the decrease in economic growth. The data also suggest an increase in the "informal sectors of labor market," such as agricultural jobs and self-employment. Between 1983-85 self employed grew by 22.4 percent while wage labor grew by 0.3 percent. See *Informe Económico 1985*, Ministerio de Planificación y Política Económica. pp. 40-41.

9. See George Westerman's 1955 study on *Urban Housing in Panama*, Panama, R.P. for an account of the poor housing condition in Calidonia, Chorrillo, Marañon, San Miguel, all communities of wooden tenements which were originally rented to West Indians working in the Canal Zone. For a current account of these and newer slum communities see Samuel Gutiérrez, *Marginalidad y viviendas, el problema de la "Barriada" en la Ciudad de Panamá*, Panama 1974.

10. Eric de León, University of Panama industrial psychologist and San Miguelito's first community planner, identified many of the owners of these lands (see *Informe sobre posesión de las tierras en San Miguelito*, prepared by Eric de León, 1971). Some still own the lands.

11. By Florentino Castro, the same individual who named San Miguelito. He thought that there were too many San Miguels in Panama, and whenever he would ask bus or taxi drivers to take him to San Miguel Adentro, they would invariably take him several kilometers south of his destination to an urban slum community by the name of San Miguel.

12. See Herasto Reyes, *Historia de San Miguelito*, p. 29.

13. Reyes, p. 31.

14. Reyes, p. 41.

15. See George Priestley, *Military Government and Popular Participation in Panama*, Westview Press, 1986. Esp. Ch. 2.

16. Reyes, p. 43.

17. Reyes, p. 50.

18. Reyes, pp. 63-75.

19. Reyes, p. 61.

20. Reyes, p. 77.

21. Priestley, *op. cit.*

22. See INCAE 1, p. 4.

23. Reyes, p. 94.

24. For an interesting synthesis of the church's doctrinal development and Latin America and the new currents and counter-currents which developed in the decade of the 1960s and 1970s see Rodolfo Casillas Ramirez, "El orden social que promueve Juan Pablo II en América Central." *CITGUA*, Cuadernos No. 9 and 3, Marzo 1986, Mexico.

25. Interview with CEASPA—Centro de Educación y Acción Social Panameña—in Panama City, January 1987.

26. See INCAE, #1, p. 5.

27. See Comisión de Estudios Interdisciplinarios para el Desarrollo de la Nacionalidad, Anexo B. Programa de Desarrollo de la Comunidad del Movimiento de Unificación Nacional, Desarrollo y Orientacion (MUNDO), December 1968.

28. Interview with Ramón Hernández, April 28, 1974.

29. See Eric de León, *Informe de la investigación realizada hasta la fecha, sobre el centro de producción de Nuevo Veranillo (CENTROCOOP).*

30. See Paul Taylor, Evaluación del programa de desarrollo comunal urbano de Panamá, Oficina de Desarrollo Comunal Urbano, Ministerio de Trabajo y Bienestar Social, Panama, Republic of Panama. See especially Ch. 10. ODCU officials complained that AID had too much control over their agency, p. 35.

31. Ramón Hernández, August 12, 1974.

32. See Herasto Reyes, *op. cit.* p. 103-104.

33. For a thorough discussion of the 1960s crisis of hegemony and the emergence of the military, see Priestley op. cit., esp. Ch. 2.

34. See *Hacia la reestructuración del país: communicado de la cuarta línea,* p. 1.

35. See Reyes, p. 109 and interviews with Father Mahon, Eric de León, and Ramón Hernández.

36. See municipal rights to tax-constitution of 1947 and 1972.

37. See Castells, *op. cit.*

38. See INCAE #1 p. 10 and for a history of the development of Community Development Agencies in Panama, see Guillermo Medina, *Desarrollo de la comunidad* 1966.

39. INCAE, *op. cit.* #1, p. 12.

40. See Gary MacEoin, "Church-State Rift Grows in Panama" *National Catholic Reporter,* Jan. 7, 1962.

41. Sociedad President Reluz, cited in INCAE, *op. cit.*, San Miguelito, #2, p. 15.

42. Interview Eric de León, August, 1973.

43. The military divided the country in 505 *corregimientos* with their respective elected representatives who became the basis of the new legitimacy.See George Priestley, *Military Government and Popular Participation in Panama, op. cit.* Ch. 5-6.

44. See Ministerio de Planificación y Política Económica, *Una década de desarrollo social en Panamá 1970-1980* (Capitulo II, Los Sectores Sociales), Panama 1984.

45. For figures see George Kourany, *op. cit.* p. 2; land reform see Stanley Heckandon Moreno, *Asentamientos campesinos*, Panama 1974.

46. P. 2 and 3 of George Kourany, Proyecciones de San Miguelito-1987, Ministerio de Vivienda.

47. In 1980 the *corregimiento* of Belisario Porras had 50% of San Miguelito's population. Belisario Porras jumped from 14,204 inhabitants in 1970 to 79,890 in 1980., Domingo Espinar was the only other *corregimiento* in San Miguelito that

registered such dramatic population increases. In 1970 it had 10,508 and in 1980 it climbed to 23,342. Therefore it is not surprising to learn that in the same decade Belisario Porras and Domingo Espinar's housing stock increased by 503% and 166% respectively. (see Kourany p. 6) The other three *corregimientos* had less dramatic increases. (Censos Nacionales 1980, Volumen VII, sectores censales de los distritos de Panamá, San Miguelito y Colón. Dirección de Estadística y Censo, Contraloría General de la República, República de Panamá. p. 132-133.)

48. Kourany, p. 9.

49. For a good review of the military government's transitional problems 1976-1984 see Guillermo Castro, *Recuento y perspectivas*, CELA 1986.

50. See Omaira Lopez and Clara A. Jeannette de Daily, *El distrito de San Miguelito: estructura socio-económica y régimen administrativo*, Thesis, University of Panama, p. 44.

51. a) Panama has 505 *corregimientos* and hence 505 local community boards. When the 505 representatives met in October of each year, they met as the National Assembly of Community Representatives. b) The constitutional reform of 1978 and 1983 substantially modified this structure of government. For example, the National Assembly of Community Representatives was abolished and replaced by a National Legislature. c) However, the local community boards are still in existence and they are still presided over by the local elected representative. For a thorough discussion of these local structures of participation, see Priestley, *op. cit.*, chapters 5 and 6.

52. For a thorough discussion of Junta Comunal-Health Committee conflicts nationwide see Priestley, Op.cit. 100-102 and for a discussion of corruption in San Miguelito see Omaira Lopez and Clara Jeannette de Daily, *El distrito de San Miguelito: estructura socio-económica y régimen administrativo*, Thesis, University of Panama, 1977 p. 55; see also interview with Father Karamenitis, 1-10-87.

53. See Omaira Lopez, Op. cit. p. 42.

54. See *Documento síntesis, programa de desarrollo urbano integral de San Miguelito*, 1981, Panama, Introduction.

55. See discussion at Primer Seminario Sobre San Miguelito, January 6-10, 1987.

56. Phase two of DIUSMI, slated for 1981-1985, was not undertaken.

57. For thorough discussion of 1984 elections see Terence W. Modglin, *Panamanian Presidential and Legislative Election: 1984*. Center for Strategic and International Studies, Georgetown University, Wash., D.C. 1984.

58. For an early analysis of the election results, see George Priestley, "Panama: Transition from Military to Civilian Government," *Everybody's Magazine*, 1984. A much more comprehensive analysis is Simeón Gonzalez, *La crisis del Torrijismo y las elecciones de 1984*, Panamá, 1985. For an account by the opposition, see Raúl Arias de Para, *Así fue el fraude*, Panamá, 1984.

59. Although the government has not published a detailed election result, a partial and incomplete result is contained in Boletín Tribunal Electoral, No. 286, Friday November 9, 1984, Panamá R. P.

60. Much of this information was gathered from careful reading of dailies and interviews with Balbina de Perinan's staff.

61. Interview with Balbina de Perinan's principal advisers, 1/87.

62. Interview with Ford—Treasurer of San Miguelito.

63. Interview with Balbina de Perinan's principal advisers, 1/87.

64. See paper presented by Tomás Sosa at Primer Encuentro de Problemas Urbanos San Miguelito, 1987.

65. This section is taken from paper delivered by Ing. Sosa at the Primer Encuentro de Desarrollo de San Miguelito, January 6-10, 1987 in San Miguelito, Panama.

66. H.R. Lucho Gómez provided a small library and the community still needs a hospital. As we prepared to go to press, Panama suffered one of its worst political crises in two decades. The political opposition, better known as ADO, spearheaded a brief business strike and civil disobedience in early June 1988 when Colonel Roberto Díaz-Herrera accused Colonel Antonio Noriega, Panama's Chief of National Defense, of engineering the 1984 electoral fraud and of killing General Omar Torrijos Herrera. Poor communities, especially San Miguelito, rioted for more than four days. And according to the Panamanian dailies, the riots were the worst in San Miguelito as the military confronted hundreds of armed and unarmed citizens. The new political situation might lead to a rapprochement between the military and the mayor of San Miguelito. FBIS reported that on June 11 the mayor, Balbina de Perinan, and "Lucho" Gómez, PRD San Miguelito Legislator, marched in San Miguelito in support of the military.

References

Alvarez Icaza M., José, "Indignación popular en Panamá: La Iglesia y el régimen militar al borde de la ruptura." Circulated by L.A.P. Service, Washington, D.C. 1971.

Aquí San Miguelito (San Miguelito's newspaper—various dates).

Arias de Para, Raúl, Así fue el fraude: las elecciones presidenciales de Panamá 1984. Panama, 1984.

Bravo, Francisco, The Parish of San Miguelito in Panama: History and Pastoral Theological Evaluation, Cuernavaca, Mexico, Centro Intercultural de Documentación, 1966.

Casillas Ramirez, Rodolfo, "El orden social que promueve Juan Pablo II en América Central." CITGUA, CUADERNOS NO. 9 ano 3, Marzo 1986, México.

Castells, Manuel, Crísis urbana y cambio social, México, Siglo XXI, 1981.

Castro, Guillermo, Recuento y perspectivas, CELA, Panamá, 1986.

CELA, *Boletín Bibliografico*. Sept.-Nov. 1986 (Panama, R.P.).

Collier, David, *Squatters and Oligarchs: Authoritarian Rule and Policy Change in Peru*, Baltimore, Johns Hopkins University Press, 1976.

Cornelius, Wayne, *Politics and the Migrant Poor in Mexico City*, Stanford University Press, 1975.

Diálogo Social, (1971-1987), Panamá.

De Diego, Ernesto, *Plan de Panamá*, Informe al I.V.U., Instituto de Vivienda y Urbanismo, Panamá, Febrero de 1968.

Dorado, Carlos, *Plan San Miguelito*, Paper read at "Primer Encuentro de Problemas Urbanas," Panama, January 1987.

ESTAMPA, Study on Transportation in Metropolitan Panama by Japan International Cooperation Agency, Panama, December 1982.

ESTAMPA II, (Estudio de factibilidad de proyectos de transporte en el área metropolitana de Panamá,) Sumario ejecutivo, Panamá, diciembre 1984.

Gómez Perez, José Antonio, William Hughes Ortega, *Desarrollo crísis, deuda y política económica en Panamá*, Universidad de Panamá, 1985.

González H., Simeón, *La crísis del Torrijismo y las elecciones de 1984*, Ediciones Horizonte, Panamá, 1985.

González, Simeón Emilio H, *Panamá 1985: De un fondomonetarismo sin mediación a una mediación fondomonetarista*, CELA, Panamá, 1985.

Gutiérrez, Samuel A., *Marginalidad y vivienda: El problema de las "barriadas brujas" en la Ciudad de Panamá*. Panamá, Tercera edición por Talleres de Editorial Litográfica, S.A., 197.

Heckandon Moreno, Stanley, "La Urbanización y la basura en la Ciudad de Panamá (1905-1985) in *Agonía de la Naturaleza*, Panama 1985.

—*Asentamientos campesinos*, Panama 1974.

Hughes, William R, Quintero, Ivan, *Quienes son los dueños de Panamá*, Panamá, Centro de Estudios y Acción Social Panameño (Serie Panamá Hoy 2), 1987.

Ickis, John, *San Miguelito: Case Studies No. 1, 2, 3, and 4*, Instituto Centroamericano de Administración de Empresas (INCAE), 1972.

Kourany, George, "Proyecciones San Miguelito 1987," Ministerio de Vivienda, Panamá Enero 1987. Panamá, R. P.

Leis, Raúl y Mariela Arace, "Aproximación al problema del transporte colectivo en la Ciudad de Panamá" in *Praxis Centroamericana*, Panamá, No. 1 (Julio/Diciembre de 1982), pp. 1-66.

De León, Eric, *Programa de Desarrollo de la Communidad del Movimiento de Unificación Nacional, Desarrollo y Orientación (MUNDO)*, Anexo B, Panama, Diciembre de 1968.

—*Informe sobre posesion de las tierras en San Miguelito*, Panamá, 1971.

—*Informe de la investigación realizada hasta la fecha, sobre el centro de producción de Nuevo Veranillo*, Panamá, nd.

Lista de asentamientos espontaneos en existencia a nivel nacional., Panamá Ministerio de Vivienda, 1986.

Los Corregimientos en el desarrollo socio-económico de Panamá, Dirección Nacional de Planeamiento y Reforma Educativa, Ministerio de Educación, Panamá, R. P. 1972.

MacEoin, Gary, "Church-State Rift Grows in Panama," *National Catholic Reporter*, January 7, 1972.

Menéndez-Carrión, Amparo, *La conquista del voto: de Velasco a Roldós*, Quito, Corporación Editora Nacional, 1986.

Ministerio de Planificación y Política Económica, *Una década de desarrollo social en Panamá 1970-1980* (Capitulo 11—Los sectores sociales), Panamá 1984.

Medina, Guillermo, *Desarrollo de la comunidad*, Panamá 1966.

—*Sobre el momento político actual*, No. 7, Panamá, 5 de Febrero de 1984.

Ministerio de Planificación y Política Económica, "La captación y los sectores informales" (Documento de Trabajo No. 39) Panamá, Sept. 1982.

—"Características de la mujer panameña en áreas marginadas, Panamá, Abril de 1983.

—Perfil del desempleo en Panamá 1979-1982.

MIPPE, Observaciones sobre el programa DUISMI-Fase 1., Panamá, 2 de Junio de 1981.

—Lista de asentamientos espontáneos en existencia a nivel nacional, Unpublished, Panama, 1986.

—various charts on migration to metropolitan region. The charts were prepared by social scientists working in the Ministerio de Planificación y Política Económica.

Mock Cedeno, Ariel, "Estudio socio-económico de los grupos poblacionales del distrito de San Miguelito," Internacionales S.A. CONAISA, Panamá, Abril 1981.

—Resumen ejecutivo y ampliaciones conceptuales de algunos aspectos de la investigación de los grupos poblacionales pobres, empresas y empresarios del distrito de San Miguelito.

—"Panamá: situación y perspectivas del empleo femenino." (Documento de Trabajo No. 21). Marzo 1984.

Muñoz B. and Florencio R, *San Miguelito: presente, pasado, futuro*, Panamá, 1985 (magazine published by Comité Ejecutivo del XV Aniversario del Distrito de San Miguelito).

Newspaper Clippings on San Miguelito 1985-86, from files of Banco Hipotecario Nacional.

Organización Internacional del Trabajo, "Panamá: situación y perspectivas del empleo en el sector informal urbano," (Documento de Trabajo No. 22) Marzo 1984.

Pacheco, Rubén D. (Director de la Secretaría Técnica de Planificación del Ministerio de Vivienda), "Vivienda y acción gubernamental en San Miguelito 1958-1986." Primer Encuentro de Problemas Urbanos-Distrito de San Miguelito, Panamá, Enero 7, 1987.

Pedro Pou, "Empleo, inversión y crecimiento económico en Panamá durante la década de los setenta" Ministerio de Planificación y Política Económica de la República de Panamá, Buenos Aires, 1984.

Perinan Hernández, Virgilio, "San Miguelito: el más joven distrito debe ser declarado área de urgencia nacional," in Diálogo Social, Panamá Año XIX (Enero de 1986), p. 21.

—"San Miguelito: problemas del distrito," *Diálogo Social*, Panamá Ano XIX, No. 186 (Febrero de 1986), p. 23.

—"San Miguelito: las invasiones, una constatación de la injusticial social y económica," *Diálogo Social*, Panamá Año XIX, No. 187, (Marzo de 1986), p. 33.

—"San Miguelito: la juventud y el desempleo," *Diálogo Social*, Panamá, Año XIX, No. 188 (Abril de 1986), p. 39.

—"San Miguelito: el desempleo," *Diálogo Social*, Panamá Año XIX, No. 189 (Mayo de 1986), p. 22.

Porcell G. Néstor, "Los niveles de pobreza en San Miguelito" in *Cuadernos de Sociología* (Departamento de Sociología), N. 1 Año. 1 1985, Panamá, Universidad de Panamá, pp. 21-63.

Priestley, George, *Military Government and Popular Participation in Panama*, Westview Press, 1986.

—"Panama: Transition from miltary to civilian government," *Everybody's Magazine*, New York, 1984.

Programa de desarrollo urbano integral de San Miguelito, DUISMI 2. (Documento Síntesis).

República de Panamá, *Decreto de Gabinete No. 147 (3 de Junio de 1969)*, decree that creates the Dirección General para el Desarrollo de la Comunidad—DIGEDECOM.

—*Decreto de Gabinete No. 222 (16 de Julio 1969)*, assigns functions to DIGEDECOM.

—*Gaceta Oficial*, Decreto de Gabinete No. 258 of 30 July 1970, creates the Experimental District of San Miguelito, R.P.

Reyes, Herasto, *Historia de San Miguelito*, Panamá, Centro de Communicación Popular, 1981.

Sanjur, Conrado, *El caso de las comunidades cristianas de base en el Distrito Especial de San Miguelito*. Panamá, 1985.

Síntesis, (magazine) Panama.

Taylor, Paul, *Evaluación del programa de desarrollo comunal urbano de Panamá*, Ministerio de Trabajo y Bienestar Social, Septiembre 1968.

The San Miguelito Paper, prepared by the priests of San Miguelito, January 20, 1964.

Torres Abrego, José Eulogio, *En torno a la crisis y la problemática actual de la economía panameña*, Panamá, Imprenta Universitaria, 1986.

Westerman, George W., *Urban Housing in Panama*, Panama, The Institute for Economic Development, May 1955.

Interviews

Hernández, Ramón, Spring of 1974 and Summer of 1974.

De León, Eric, Summer of 1971 and Summer of 1973.

Mahon, Father Leon of the Parish of San Miguelito, Summer 1973 and Summer 1974.

Father Karamenitis of *Corregimiento* of Belisario Porras, San Miguelito, Jan. 1987.

Donadio, A., Assistant to the Mayor of San Miguelito, Jan. 1987.

Perignan, Virgilio, Political Adviser to the Mayor of San Miguelito, Jan. 1987.

Kourany, George, Principal Adviser to the Minister of Housing, Jan. 1987.

Ford, A. San Miguelito's Planning Officer, 1987. Treasurer of the Municipality of San Miguelito, 1987. Bureau Chief of Asentamientos Espontáneos, Ministry of Housing, 1987.

Letters, Communiques, Speeches, Newspapers, Decrees

Comunicado de la Conferencia Episcopal Panameña, document signed by Archbishop Marcos McGrath and several Panamanian bishops, June 14, 1971.

Hacia una reestructuracion del país: Comunicado de la cuarta linea, published by Mundo, November 1968.

De León, Eric, *Informe sobre posesión de las tierras en San Miguelito,* 1971.

INDEX